CW00428928

Laurence Main

Kittiwake Press in association with John Bartholomew & Son Ltd

Published by
The Kittiwake Press in association with
John Bartholomew & Son Ltd,
Duncan Street, Edinburgh EH9 1TA

Editor: David Perrott

Photographs: Laurence Main

Drawings: Morag Perrott

Dedicated to Chantal Gwyneth

Special thanks to Janet Davies, Joseph Jones, Tom Jones, Mrs
Hayley Turner (née Griffiths) and Margaret Hughes

Typesetting: Perrott Cartographics, Darowen, Machynlleth
and Litho Link, Welshpool

Origination: Litho Link, Welshpool

Printing and binding: Richard Clay, Bungay, Suffolk

Front cover: Fron-goch from Cefncoch Isaf: Laurence Main

ISBN 0 7028 0887 3

1/3.0/4-88

Introduction

The Dyfi Valley is one of the most beautiful valleys in Wales. Traditionally the frontier between north and south Wales, it is where the counties of Gwynedd, Powys and Dyfed meet today. As the river winds the 30 miles from its source to the sea it passes through a surprising variety of scenery, with its tributaries encouraging you to take a wider view from the surrounding ridges and hills.

There is no better way of exploring this area than on foot. The bulk of the guide consists of a strip map at a scale of 4 inches to 1 mile, marking in such details as stiles, gates and signposts, while a walk profile gives an impression of the ups and downs. Information about public transport, accommodation, shops and cafés is included. There are notes on interesting places to visit, and plenty of photographs and drawings.

Read the strip map from the bottom to the top of each page (when walking from Aberdyfi to Borth), so that the map faces the direction in which you walk. As this means that north cannot always be at the top of the page, the direction of north is shown in red on each page. The sheet number of the relevant Ordnance Survey Landranger map is also given, so that the strip map can be related to the surrounding countryside.

The Dyfi Valley Way makes an ideal week's backpacking holiday. It is just as enjoyable, however, when split into short sections and walked at convenient intervals. In addition to more stiles and signposts, it is hoped eventually to mark The Way using a distinctive waymark — a dove.

Order of content

'A day's walking; a week's good health.'
(French proverb).

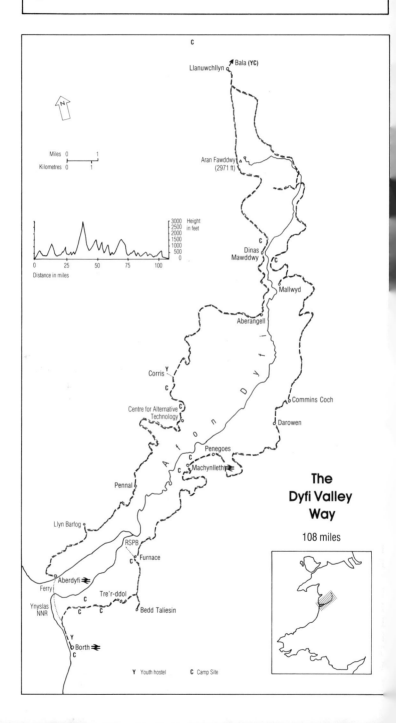

The
**Dyfi Valley
Way**

108 miles

Mileage and facilities chart

Place	Page	Mile	Train	Bus	Campsite	Youth Hostel	B&B	Shop	Café	Post Office	Bank	Launderette	Early Closing Day
Aberdyfi	7	0	BR	✔			✔	✔	✔	✔	✔		W
Pennal	13	8		✔			✔	✔		✔			W
Pantperthog	17	16		✔	✔				✔				
Corris	20	19	NG	✔	✔	✔	✔	✔	✔	✔			W
Aberllefenni	22	21		✔				✔					W
Aberangell	26	27		✔				✔		✔			
Dinas Mawddwy	31	31		✔	✔		✔	✔	✔	✔	F		T
Llanuwchllyn	41	43	NG	✔	✔	B	✔	✔	B	✔	B		W
Dinas Mawddwy	55	61		✔	✔		✔	✔	✔	✔	F		T
Mallwyd	57	63		✔			✔	✔	✔	✔			
Gwalia	64	74					✔						
Commins Coch	65	75		✔				✔		✔			T
Cefncoch uchaf	65	76					✔						
Darowen	67	77		P			✔						
Penegoes	73	85		✔					✔	✔			
Machynlleth	77	87	BR	✔	✔			✔	✔	✔	✔	✔	T
Furnace	84	97		✔	✔		E	E	✔				
Tre'r-ddol	88	102		✔				✔	✔				
Llancynfelyn	89	104			✔								
Borth	92	108	BR	✔		✔	✔	✔	✔	✔	✔	✔	W

B&B — Bed and breakfast in farmhouse, guest house or hotel
BR — British Rail
NG — Narrow gauge railway
P — Postbus
B — Proceed to Bala by train or bus
E — At Eglwys Fach
F — Fridays only
T — Thursdays
W — Wednesdays

6 Aberdyfi

Aberdyfi means the mouth of the Dyfi. This delightful village is situated on a sandy foreshore on the northern side of the Dyfi estuary where the river flows into Cardigan Bay. Charles Dibdin made the village famous when he composed the song 'The Bells of Aberdovey' in 1785. It was sung by a comic Welsh character in Dibden's Drury Lane hit 'Liberty Hall' and was later associated with Madam Edith Wynne, the 'Welsh Nightingale'. It is the stories of the bells that are most enchanting, however. One story is that Idris Gawr, a giant who used to sit on Cadair Idris (hence its name — Idris' chair), carried a huge bell. He used to paddle in the river Dyfi but was drowned in a storm and his great bell lost in the sands, still to be heard at times. A more modern tale is that the bells were brought from Flanders to Aberdyfi church tower, but the ship carrying them was threatened in a storm before the heavy bells could be landed, so they were dumped overboard as a safety precaution. This story is hard to swallow Aberdyfi didn't have its own church until after Dibdin's death in 1814. More likely is the one about bells being tied around the necks of sheep in the ancient past, as with modern Swiss cows. Menna, a shepherdess, sang to their accompaniment as she kept watch for her sailor lover to return. The favourite story, however, is of 'Cantre'r Gwaelod' or the 'Lowland Hundred', a once fertile plain now covered by Cardigan Bay. According to legend, this most fertile part of the Lord of Ceredigion's land was drowned in the 6thC AD. This undoubtedly happened, although modern geologists date the event as no later than 3500 BC. Remains of tree stumps of submerged forests can still be seen. There are distinctive submerged reefs bordering this area to the south and north to mark its possible boundaries, Sarn y Bwch near Tywyn and Sarn Cynfelin between Borth and Aberystwyth.

The seaward side of 'Cantre'r Gwaelod' had to be protected by strong walls or dykes. Gwyddno Garanhir, Lord of Ceredigion, entrusted these defences to Seithennin, but this notorious drunkard neglected his duty and a storm broke the walls while he was at a feast. The whole area was inundated and Manua, the chief settlement which contained the bells, drowned. Taliesin the bard escaped, as did Gwyddno, but Seithennin perished and his sons had to atone for his misdeeds, becoming Celtic saints and founding churches. (continued on page 8).

The Bells of Aberdovey

If thou truly dost love me ..
As I truly do love thee,
To all who live on land or main,
Say the bells of Aberdovey;
One, two, three, four, five, six,
Join us in a merry strain,
Say the bells of Aberdovey.

Listen to the joyous bells,
While through the meadows straying,
O'er the hills their music swells,
And this is what they're saying:

Pretty maidens, come again ..
Join us in a merry strain,
To all who live on land or main,
Say the bells of Aberdovey,
One, two, three, four, five, six,
Join us in a merry strain
Say the bells of Aberdovey.

Sunshine gilds the lovely dolls,
And little birds are singing,
Lads are listening to the bells,
And they are ever ringing,

Pretty maidens etc.

While the fitful changing moon
Is shining on the river,
They will never change their tune,
But ring their chime for ever:

Pretty maidens etc.

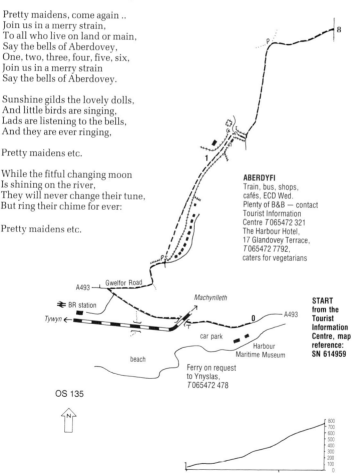

ABERDYFI
Train, bus, shops,
cafés, ECD Wed.
Plenty of B&B — contact
Tourist Information
Centre *T* 065472 321
The Harbour Hotel,
17 Glandovey Terrace,
T 065472 7792,
caters for vegetarians

A493 — Gwelfor Road

BR station

Tywyn ←

Machynlleth

A493

car park

Harbour
Maritime Museum

beach

Ferry on request
to Ynyslas,
T 065472 478

OS 135

N

**START
from the
Tourist
Information
Centre, map
reference:
SN 614959**

8 Above Aberdyfi

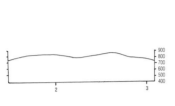

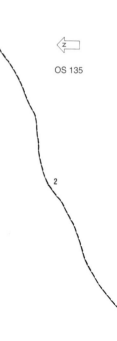

OS 135

Aberdyfi's isolated position has encouraged history to pass it by, although it seems always to have been an important crossing point from north to south Wales. In 1216, Llywellyn ap Iorwerth called all Welsh rulers to the Great Council of Aberdyfi, in an attempt to unite Wales. Only 3 houses were recorded at 'Devye' in 1569, but herring fishermen from all parts assembled here in season. Great excitement was caused by the arrival of a Spanish ship in 1597. The Spaniards landed on a foraging expedition and defence forces hurriedly mustered to pick off some sailors with musket shots before the Spaniards sailed away.

The local oak forests, now denuded, provided timber for export, while the fish landed here fed southern Meirionnydd in the famine year of 1649. The 18thC saw the growth of lead, silver, zinc and copper exports. Some of these minerals came from Aberdyfi itself. The Company of Mine Adventurers was recorded as shipping lead and copper from Aberdovey in 1708. In 1823 a copper mine was available for leasing just 500 yards from the Dyfi's bank. By then, however, the mineral industry was in decline. The last record of mining in Aberdyfi was the sale of Corbet Dovey copper mine in 1863. This mine was so close to the shore that its ore was loaded directly onto the boats.

The wool trade replaced minerals for a while, but the industrialisation of this industry in Yorkshire halted this development. Instead, the mid 19thC saw the rapid growth of Aberdyfi as a port. Shipbuilding was a thriving local industry, while many locals went to sea, giving Aberdyfi its strong maritime influence, as recorded by the Rev. D.W. Morgan in his book '*Brief Glory*,' and by the Maritime Museum on the sea front which is run by the local Outward Bound Centre, started here during the Second World War.

(Continued on page 9)

The railway reached the southern side of the Dyfi estuary in 1864, heralding the start of the tourist industry. A ferry from the Ynyslas shore transported passengers to Aberdyfi, as it had for centuries. There were plans to bridge the estuary at this point, but the railway finally reached Aberdyfi from Dyfi Junction in 1867, when it was stipulated that the fare from Aberdyfi to Ynyslas (station now closed, but close to Borth) should reflect the former distance by ferry and not the actual rail mileage. A railway line had reached Aberdyfi from the north in 1863, allowing slate from Abergynolwyn to be exported from Aberdyfi harbour (via Tywyn). A 373 ft long jetty allowed ships to be loaded and unloaded even at low tide, while prospects of Aberdyfi becoming an Irish ferry port were provided by the Aberdyfi and Waterford Steamship Co. Ltd, whose services also imported Irish cattle and potatoes. A lifeboat was stationed here and has made several rescues over the years.

Aberdyfi's maritime tradition and its new intake of tourists were catered for by an annual regatta, the first being held here in August 1880. A golf course opened and local families were known to camp out in July and August to release their properties for tourist income. The village grew to boast 1358 inhabitants in 310 houses in 1901. The church, which wasn't built until 1842 (until then worshippers had to travel to Tywyn) finally had its bells installed in 1937. Tourism now reigned supreme, with there being no place for a small port in the fiercely competitive 20thC. The Outward Bound Centre is a reminder of the past, however, while a ferry still takes tourists across to Ynyslas during the season. The Snowdonia National Park maintains a Tourist Information Centre, and the Seafront Garden Project earned Aberdyfi the Prince of Wales Award for Environmental Improvement in 1972.

Photo: Aberdyfi.

At Carn March Arthur we find reminders of King Arthur for the first (but not the last) time on this walk. Carn March Arthur is a rock indented with what is said to be the hoofprint of Arthur's horse. Some say the horse carried Arthur to safety from here to Ynys-hir by leaping across the Dyfi estuary when pursued by his enemies, or that the mark was left after King Arthur's horse had dragged a large, hairy monster out of Llyn Barfog, the nearby lake. Others say it was Huw Gadarn, or Hu the Mighty, who captured a local monster and dragged it into the lake, where it was drowned. This Huw Gadarn is as interesting a character as Arthur, for he is said to have led the first colony of Cymri into Britain from Defrobane, where Istanbul now stands, in about 1800 BC. The educational system of the druids is traced to Huw Gadarn, who is said to have mnemonically systematised the wisdom of the ancestors of those people whom he had led west. He was regarded as the personification of intellectual culture and is commemorated for having made poetry the vehicle of memory and to have invented the Triads. To him is attributed the founding of Stonehenge and the introduction of glass-making and writing in Ogham characters. An ox was depicted on his standard, perhaps depicting the sign of Taurus and being the origin of the sobriquet 'John Bull'. He established that a Gorsedd or assembly of druids and bards must be held on an open, uncovered, grass space, in a conspicuous place in full view and hearing of the people. Llyn Barfog means the Bearded Lake. This may refer to the flowery covering on the surface of the lake (water-lilies could be in flower any time from late June to early September), although it is said to commemorate one of King Arthur's knights — 'the bearded one'. Barfog may even refer to King Arthur's foster-father. The lake is most famous for a fairy-tale, however. The story takes various forms, but the essence is that a fairy-cow from the Llyn Barfog area came into the possession of a poor farmer from Dysyrnant (½ mile north of the lake). It bore him fine calves, gave plenty of rich milk and brought luck and wealth. When the cow grew old, however, the farmer decided to slaughter her. When the time came, the knife fell from the hand of the butcher and from the rocks above the lake a little green fairy woman called the cow home. The cow and her calves disappeared into the lake along with the fairy woman and the farmer soon found his luck had deserted him.

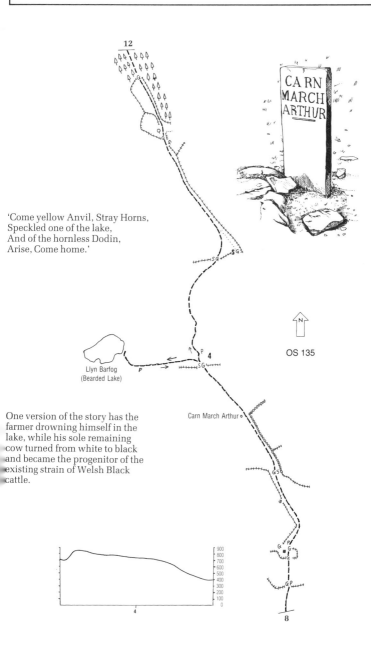

12

CARN
MARCH
ARTHUR

'Come yellow Anvil, Stray Horns,
Speckled one of the lake,
And of the hornless Dodin,
Arise, Come home.'

N

OS 135

Llyn Barfog
(Bearded Lake)

4

Carn March Arthur

One version of the story has the
farmer drowning himself in the
lake, while his sole remaining
cow turned from white to black
and became the progenitor of the
existing strain of Welsh Black
cattle.

900
800
700
600
500
400
300
200
100
0

4

8

Pennal is an ancient site. The Romans built a fort to accommodate a garrison of 500 men at Cefn-caer, 600 yards south-east of the present village. This fort was on Sarn Helen, the Roman road from Caerhun, near Conwy, to Moridunium (Carmarthen), and occupied a strategic ridge 50 feet above the river's floodplain, which surrounded it on three sides, and near an ancient ford. It could be conveniently served from the sea by way of the Dyfi estuary. Roman coins, a gold chain, bricks, pottery and tiles have been found here and Roman bricks were visible in the walls of Pennal church before it was demolished in 1769 prior to rebuilding. The circular graveyard indicates an ancient pre-Christian site. Remains of a Roman hypocaust were also found at Cefn-caer in 1865 but little remains now, just grassy banks with a farmhouse set in what was the west corner of the fort. This may have been Maglona where a Thracian cavalry unit were settled.

The Tomen Las or Green Mound between Pennal and Talgarth is probably the site of a medieval llys or court. Owain Glyndŵr summoned a parliament here in 1404 which agreed to place the Welsh church's allegiance to the French-backed Avignon pope Benedict XIII. St David's, now an archbishopric, was free of Canterbury's dominance, while universities were planned for both north and south Wales.

Look for a memorial plaque erected in the village to honour the six crew members of an RAF Wellington bomber, based at Moreton-in-Marsh, Glos, who died when their plane crashed into Ffridd Rhosfarch, the hillside above Pennal, on August 17th, 1941, at 11.40, while on a routine cross-country training flight in low cloud.

13 Pennal

6

A493

Aberdyfi

OS 135

N

400
300
200
100
0

5   6

Cefn-cynhafal

5

11

Pennal church hall houses an interesting exhibition of the village's history. Ask the rector for the key to see it. The rectory is the last house on the left as the A493 leaves Pennal for Machynlleth. The church hall is near the war memorial (and plaque).

Ask the farmer's (Mr Rowlands) permission before visiting the site of Cefn-caer (Roman fort).

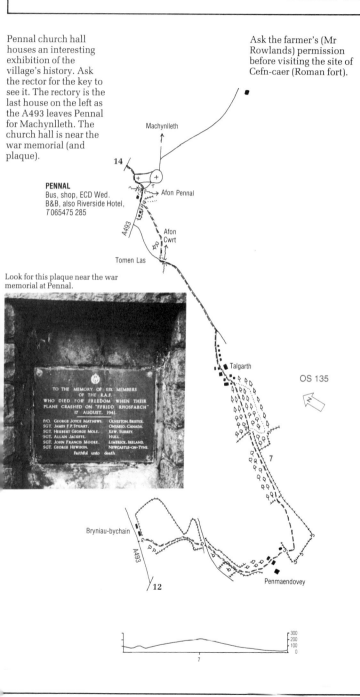

Machynlleth

14

PENNAL
Bus, shop, ECD Wed.
B&B, also Riverside Hotel,
☎ 065475 285

A493

Afon Pennal

Afon Cwrt

Tomen Las

Look for this plaque near the war memorial at Pennal.

Talgarth

OS 135

7

Bryniau-bychain

A493

12

Penmaendovey

300
200
100
0

7

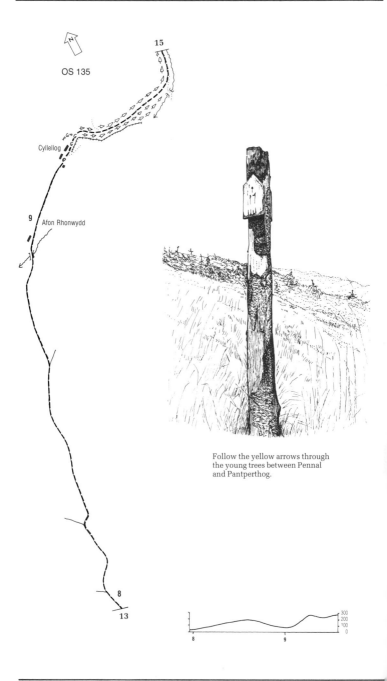

OS 135

15

Cylleliog

9 Afon Rhonwydd

8

13

Follow the yellow arrows through the young trees between Pennal and Pantperthog.

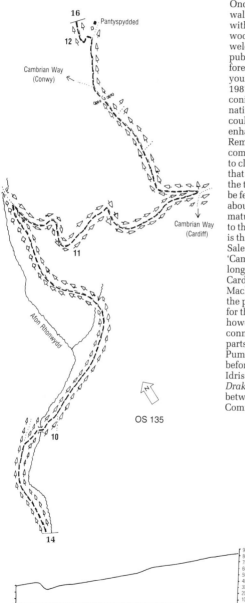

Once past the gate in the wall the path is waymarked with yellow arrows on wooden posts. This is a welcome sign of respect for public paths from the foresters, although the young trees growing here in 1987 were still the alien conifers, rather than the native deciduous trees that could do so much to enhance the environment. Remember that these commercial forests are prone to clear felling, which means that what are mature trees at the time of writing may soon be felled. These conifers take about 40 years to grow to maturity. The track going off to the left just after the gate is the route taken by Richard Sale's version of the 'Cambrian Way', a 260 mile long distance path from Cardiff to Conwy via Machynlleth. Tony Drake is the person most responsible for the Cambrian Way idea, however, and his 'mountain connoisseurs' 274 mile walk parts from Richard Sale's at Pumlumon, going eastwards before rejoining it at Cadair Idris. We shall share *Tony Drake's* 'Cambrian Way' between Mallwyd and Commins Coch.

Go over this stile and down to
Pantperthog.

You are on the
slopes of your
first mountain,
the 2186 ft
Tarren y Gesail

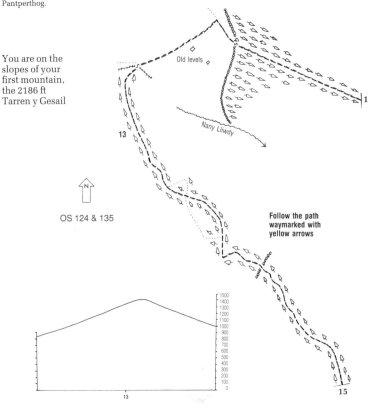

Old levels

Nany Lliwdy

13

OS 124 & 135

Follow the path
waymarked with
yellow arrows

17

15

13

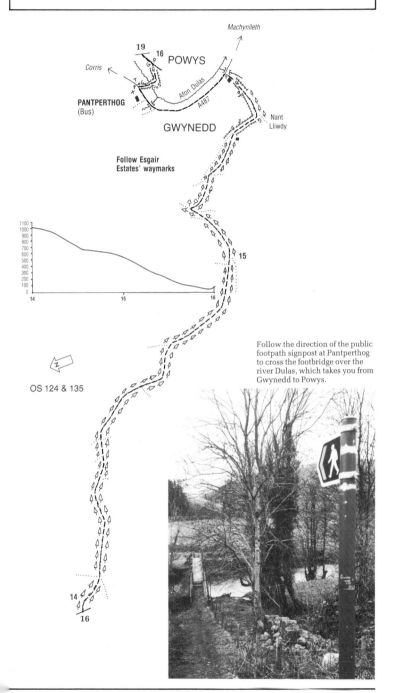

Machynlleth

19 **16** POWYS

Corris

Afon Dulas

A487

PANTPERTHOG
(Bus)

GWYNEDD

Nant
Lliwdy

**Follow Esgair
Estates' waymarks**

1100
1000
900
800
700
600
500
400
300
200
100
0

14   15   16

15

OS 124 & 135

Follow the direction of the public
footpath signpost at Pantperthog
to cross the footbridge over the
river Dulas, which takes you from
Gwynedd to Powys.

14
16

18 Centre for Alternative Technology

The Centre for Alternative Technology, or simply 'The Quarry', is a prime attraction on this route. Over 50,000 people visit it each year, coming from all corners of the world. Set in the derelict Llwyngwern Quarry, it is an award winning show place, testing ground and resource centre for a more environmentally sensitive lifestyle. Priority is given to energy conservation and avoiding pollution, so walkers are especially welcome. Exhibits range from wind generators and solar panels to a conservation house which proves that investment in insulation is well worthwhile. The organic vegetable garden is a great favourite, being established on unpromising soil yet flourishing with the aid of natural fertilisers and composts. Wholefood meals and snacks are available in the restaurant, while children have a special play area. Perhaps the most significant displays for the rambler are those to do with woodland and biofuel, for here is a glimpse of a sustainable future that could lead to the restoration of Wales' natural climax vegetation, the native deciduous trees. Include a visit to the well-stocked bookshop and pick up a leaflet on short residential courses on subjects ranging from low-cost building to vegetarian cookery. 'The Quarry' is a living community, not a museum, with a broad appeal.

Photo: Solar energy panels at the Centre for Alternative Technology.

B&B & campsite at
Y Goedwig, Corris,
SY20 9RD, *T*065473 203

ESGAIR-GEILIOG

20
18

A487
(bus)

The Organic Garden, Centre for
Alternative Technology.

Afon Dulas (county boundary)

17

OS 135 & 124

■ Plas Llwyngwern

Llwyngwern Farm
campsite, *T*0654 2492

**CENTRE FOR
ALTERNATIVE
TECHNOLOGY**
Open daily (ex
Christmas) 10-5
or an hour before
dusk in winter. Café

A487
(bus)

A windmill at the Centre for
Alternative Technology.

17

300
200
100
0

16   17   18

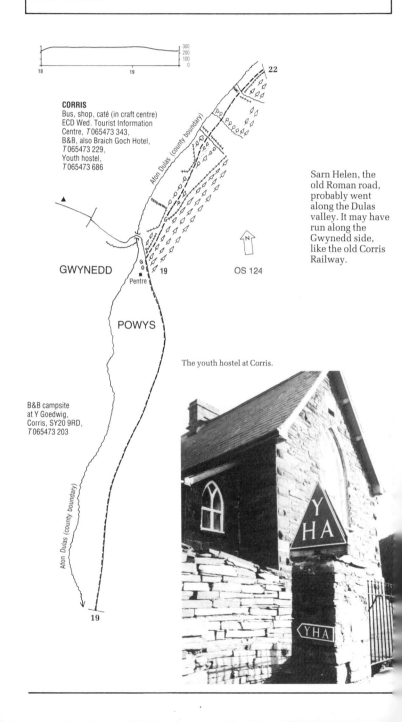

CORRIS
Bus, shop, café (in craft centre)
ECD Wed. Tourist Information
Centre, *T* 065473 343,
B&B, also Braich Goch Hotel,
T 065473 229,
Youth hostel,
T 065473 686

Aton Dulas (county boundary)

GWYNEDD

19

Pentre

POWYS

OS 124

Sarn Helen, the
old Roman road,
probably went
along the Dulas
valley. It may have
run along the
Gwynedd side,
like the old Corris
Railway.

B&B campsite
at Y Goedwig,
Corris, SY20 9RD,
T 065473 203

Aton Dulas (county boundary)

19

The youth hostel at Corris.

21 Corris

Photo: An old quarry engine is mounted in the gardens at the Corris Craft Centre.

Corris is most famous for its slates, indeed its name may even be a Welsh corruption of the English word 'quarries'. The Romans may have quarried for slate here as Sarn Helen (Roman road) seems to have passed nearby. There is a youth hostel in the old school, much frequented by those intending to walk up Cadair Idris from the Talyllyn side. If you have the time, this would make a worthwhile diversion. You should certainly visit the Corris Railway Museum. A narrow-gauge railway used to carry the slates from here to the main line at Machynlleth. It first opened as a tramway worked by horses in 1859, when it continued past Machynlleth to the old port of Derwenlas. Steam engines were introduced in 1879 and a passenger service started in 1883. The Great Western Railway, who had an interest in the competing Crosville buses, suspended passenger services just a year after taking over the line in 1930. Flood damage to the bridge over the Dyfi brought closure in 1948. The Corris Railway Society was formed in 1967 and enough track had been relaid by 1985 to run trains again on selected summer Saturdays. There are a number of interesting craft workshops in the Corris Craft Centre, whose beehive buildings lie beside the A487 above the village. The dominant industry now is forestry and The Way takes in the Foel Friog forest trail as it proceeds up the Dulas valley to the Dyfi Forest.

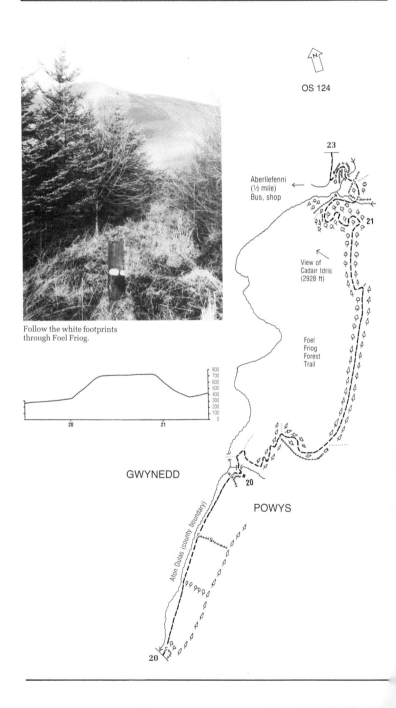

Follow the white footprints
through Foel Friog.

OS 124

23

Aberllefenni
(½ mile)
Bus, shop

21

View of
Cadair Idris
(2928 ft)

Foel
Friog
Forest
Trail

GWYNEDD

Afon Dulas (county boundary)

POWYS

20

20

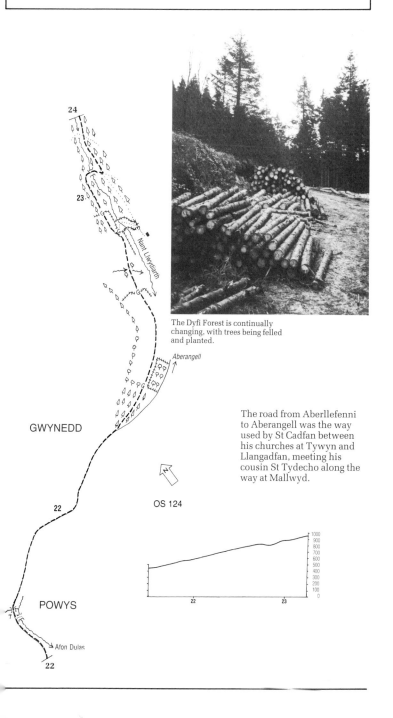

The Dyfi Forest is continually changing, with trees being felled and planted.

24

23

Nant Llwydiarth

Aberangell

GWYNEDD

POWYS

Afon Dulas

22

22

OS 124

The road from Aberllefenni to Aberangell was the way used by St Cadfan between his churches at Tywyn and Llangadfan, meeting his cousin St Tydecho along the way at Mallwyd.

1000
900
800
700
600
500
400
300
200
100
0

22   23

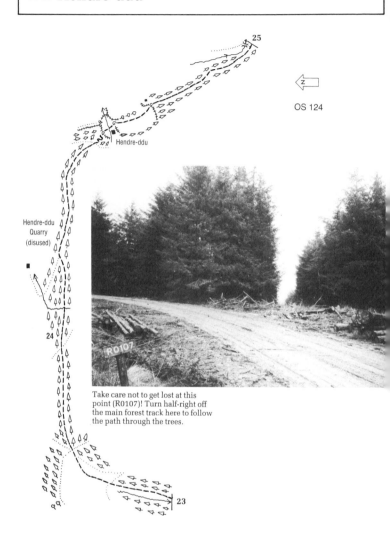

OS 124

25

Hendre-ddu

Hendre-ddu
Quarry
(disused)

24

R0107

23

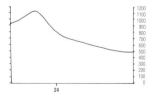

Take care not to get lost at this
point (R0107)! Turn half-right off
the main forest track here to follow
the path through the trees.

Sir Edmund Buckley established
the Hendre-ddu Slate & Slab
Company and invested large sums
in machinery and quarters for his
men at the quarry. A tramway was
built to join the Mawddwy Railway
at Aberangell and an average of 175
tons of finished slate was being
produced each month by 1876.

26

GWYNEDD

POWYS

Track bed
of old
Hendre-ddu
Tramway

Afon Angell

Aberllefenni

OS 124
or 125

26

26

25

24

The bed of the old Hendre-ddu
tramway makes a fine track beside
the river Angell.

500
400
300
200
100
0

25   26

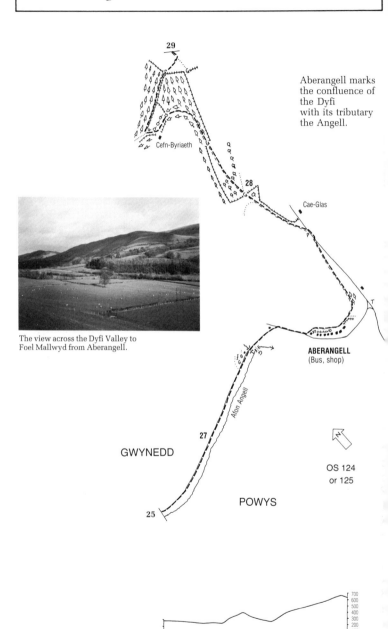

Aberangell marks
the confluence of
the Dyfi
with its tributary
the Angell.

Cefn-Byriaeth

Cae-Glas

28

29

The view across the Dyfi Valley to
Foel Mallwyd from Aberangell.

ABERANGELL
(Bus, shop)

Afon Angell

27

GWYNEDD

25

POWYS

N

OS 124
or 125

Craig y Gamell is in the background as the Afon Dyfi flows round to Pont Mallwyd.

You are about to walk across the site of King Arthur's last battle, at Camlan. The actual field is Maes-y-Camlan, just before Nant y Gamell (the Crooked Stream, rendered as 'Camel' in English), which flows into the nearby Afon Dyfi. The battle probably took place about 570 AD (allowing for the Celtic church's Gnostic practice of dating from the crucifixion and not from Jesus' birth) and was fought between Arthur and his treacherous son and nephew Mordred. Dinas Mawddwy was then part of Maelgwn Gwynedd's territory and Maelgwn is identified with Sir Lancelot. The local tradition for the battle being here is very strong and is supported by place name and other evidence. The battlefield, Maes-y-Camlan, reaches down to the Dyfi, on the other side of which is Bryn Cleifion, or hillside of the wounded. Above this is Cae'r-gof, some defensive fortifications near the old Roman road which leads towards Nant Saeson, or Saxon stream, where Mordred's Saxon allies camped the night before the battle. Arthur has other connections with this area which we shall come across later — Rhita Gawr and Aran Benllyn, Sir Cai and Caer Gai, while St Tydecho, Mawddwy's patron saint, was Arthur's nephew. The Romans are believed to have mined lead at Blaencywarch, while their road probably crossed the Dyfi where the 17thC backhorse bridge (Pont Minllyn) still stands. Locals say a castle once stood here too — could this be the dinas in Dinas Mawddwy? In 1875 during drainage operations behind the Buckley Arms Hotel, an urn was found which contained incinerated bones. Two other urns were said to have been found earlier at the old railway station, now part of Meirion Mill. Local papers of the time tell us that the urn 'was found near to the place where it is state, in some histories, that a castle stood in former years'.

The Pen-y-bont waterfall, near Pont Mallwyd.

Dinas means a fort or city, while the name Mawddwy may refer to Amwn Ddu, the father of Tydecho, patron saint of Mawddwy. Amwn Ddu married Anna, a daughter of Meurig ab Tewdrig and a sister of King Arthur, making Tydecho Arthur's nephew. It is more likely that the name is even older, however, and refers to Mawdd, a Celtic goddess. Guarded by its mountains, this area has always been a sanctuary and an independent enclave on the fringe of other areas. Mawddwy must have formed part of Maelgwn Gwynedd's territory in the 6thC as he granted St Tydecho land here as a sanctuary. It was part of Powys in the middle ages, however, and did not form part of Merioneth when the county was constituted by the Statute of Rhuddlan in 1284. It wasn't transferred from the Border Marches to Merioneth until the reign of Henry VIII. Remote bureaucrats don't seem to have cut much ice with the people of Mawddwy, however, as what they didn't have officially they assumed unofficially. The very legal existence of the 'borough' was doubted in the 19thC and a Charity Commission enquiry in 1894 concluded that the 'borough' had been a mere plaything of the Mytton family, who had come into possession of the lordship of Mawddwy by marriage about the time that it was transferred to Merioneth. Appropriately, the Myttons were descended from Hedd Mdwynog, one of the fifteen tribes of Gwynedd, while Richard Mytton became High Sheriff of Merioneth in 1542. The last of the line was the eccentric 'Mad Jack Mytton', who was born in 1796. Perhaps the most harmless of his pranks was to offer the local children half a crown to roll down Foel Dinas. At other times he deliberately overturned a gig he was driving so that his nervou friend should have first-hand experience of such a crash. He later rode a bear into his drawing-room in full hunting costume He died in a debtors' prison at the age of 38.

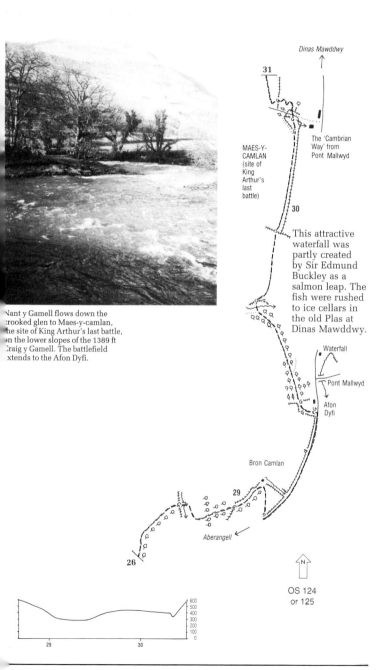

Nant y Gamell flows down the crooked glen to Maes-y-camlan, the site of King Arthur's last battle, on the lower slopes of the 1389 ft Craig y Gamell. The battlefield extends to the Afon Dyfi.

Dinas Mawddwy

31

MAES-Y-CAMLAN
(site of King Arthur's last battle)

The 'Cambrian Way' from Pont Mallwyd

30

This attractive waterfall was partly created by Sir Edmund Buckley as a salmon leap. The fish were rushed to ice cellars in the old Plas at Dinas Mawddwy.

Waterfall

Pont Mallwyd

Afon Dyfi

Bron Camlan

29

Aberangell

26

OS 124 or 125

600
500
400
300
200
100
0

29   30

The lordship of Mawddwy eventually became the property of Sir Edmund Buckley in 1856. About this time, George Borrow passed through, recording in his *'Wild Wales'* (published 1862) that 'Dinas, though at one time a place of considerable importance, if we may judge from its name which signifies a fortified city, is at present little more than a collection of filthy huts. But though a dirty, squalid place, I found it anything but silent and deserted. Fierce looking red-haired men, who seemed as if they might be descendants of the red-haired bandits of old, were staggering about, and sounds of drunken revelry echoed from the huts. I subsequently learned that Dinas was the headquarters of miners, the neighbourhood abounding with mines both of lead and stone'. Dinas had indeed been a much more important place, with a population of well over 1000, 12 shops, 14 public houses and several fairs (there were 5 fairs a year in 1680). Thousands of cattle were sold here, attracting visitors from far afield, some of whom no doubt found themselves in the Great Fetter or 'Feg Fawr'. This was an instrument for punishing drunkenness peculiar to Dinas Mawddwy and which offenders especially dreaded. Sir Edmund Buckley re-invigorated the place, investing his family's wealth, which had been gained in Manchester. The old manor house was pulled down and a noble mansion, Plas Dinas, built in its place. The Mawddwy Railway connected Dinas with the Cambrian Railway at Cemmaes Road, seven miles away, in 1868. Such was the vision of the Victorian railway pioneers that it was planned to extend the line to join the GWR at Llanuwchllyn, tunnelling under the Arans! Unfortunately, Sir Edmund Buckley overreached himself and had to file a petition at Manchester County Court for liquidation of his affairs in 1876. The family continued to live in Plas Dinas until 1900, but a fire in 1917 burnt the mansion down.

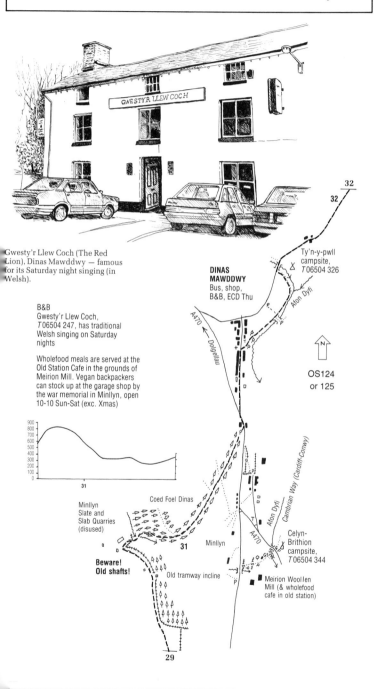

Gwesty'r Llew Coch (The Red Lion), Dinas Mawddwy — famous for its Saturday night singing (in Welsh).

B&B
Gwesty'r Llew Coch, *T*06504 247, has traditional Welsh singing on Saturday nights

Wholefood meals are served at the Old Station Cafe in the grounds of Meirion Mill. Vegan backpackers can stock up at the garage shop by the war memorial in Minllyn, open 10-10 Sun-Sat (exc. Xmas)

DINAS MAWDDWY
Bus, shop, B&B, ECD Thu

Ty'n-y-pwll campsite, *T*06504 326

Afon Dyfi

A470 ← Dolgellau

OS124 or 125

Coed Foel Dinas

Minllyn Slate and Slab Quarries (disused)

Beware! Old shafts!

Old tramway incline

Minllyn

Cambrian Way (Cardiff-Conwy)

Afon Dyfi

A470

Celyn-Brithion campsite, *T*06504 344

Meirion Woollen Mill (& wholefood cafe in old station)

31

29

32

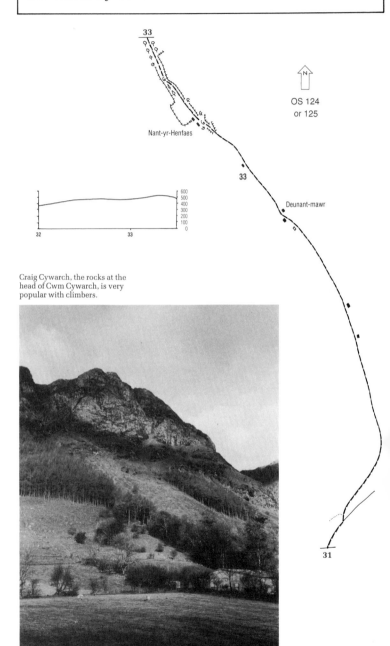

Nant-yr-Henfaes

OS 124
or 125

33

Deunant-mawr

Craig Cywarch, the rocks at the
head of Cwm Cywarch, is very
popular with climbers.

31

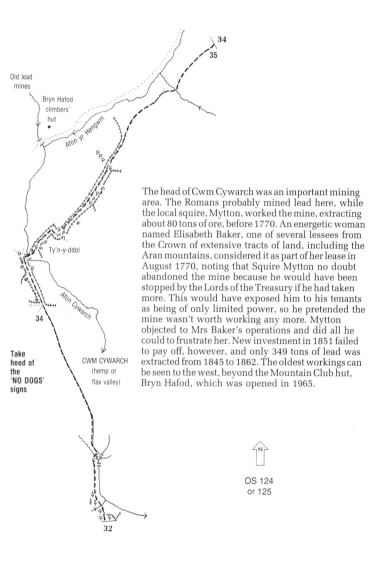

The head of Cwm Cywarch was an important mining area. The Romans probably mined lead here, while the local squire, Mytton, worked the mine, extracting about 80 tons of ore, before 1770. An energetic woman named Elisabeth Baker, one of several lessees from the Crown of extensive tracts of land, including the Aran mountains, considered it as part of her lease in August 1770, noting that Squire Mytton no doubt abandoned the mine because he would have been stopped by the Lords of the Treasury if he had taken more. This would have exposed him to his tenants as being of only limited power, so he pretended the mine wasn't worth working any more. Mytton objected to Mrs Baker's operations and did all he could to frustrate her. New investment in 1851 failed to pay off, however, and only 349 tons of lead was extracted from 1845 to 1862. The oldest workings can be seen to the west, beyond the Mountain Club hut, Bryn Hafod, which was opened in 1965.

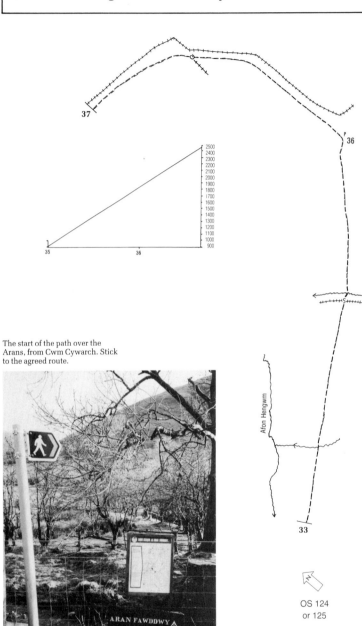

37

2500
2400
2300
2200
2100
2000
1900
1800
1700
1600
1500
1400
1300
1200
1100
1000
900

35

36

36

The start of the path over the
Arans, from Cwm Cywarch. Stick
to the agreed route.

Afon Hengwm

33

OS 124
or 125

ARAN FAWDDWY
ARAN BENLLYN

Aran Fawddwy is 2971 ft high. Although obviously a strenuous climb, it is well worth the effort, and on a fine day it is a real joy. The climb is never difficult (but keep close to the fence at Drws Bach) and is open to all with the stamina. The most important thing is to choose your weather and be prepared for any sudden deterioration. This means carrying spare warm, wind and rain proof clothing, emergency food rations and having the good sense to turn back if necessary. You must also wear good walking boots, carry a map and compass, and have left word of where you are going and when you expect to be back. This route is straightforward, having the aid of convenient fences for navigation.

Aran Fawddwy is regaining its popularity with walkers after access problems in the early 1980s. The establishment of courtesy paths, which are marked on maps displayed at the start of the climb and along the route, have led to stiles for erection over fences being air-lifted to a height of nearly 3000 ft. There are warning notices about dogs and it is *most important* that these are heeded. The Animals Act 1971 states that dogs endangering livestock may be shot. The Protection of Livestock Act 1953 makes it an offence to permit a dog to worry livestock, with a maximum penalty of £200. Worrying includes being at large in a field in which there are sheep.

As you reach Drws Bach, the 'little door' which gives access to Aran Fawddwy, notice the cairn built by members of RAF St Athan mountain rescue team in memory of SAC Mike Aspain, who on 5th June, 1960, was killed by lightning near this spot whilst on duty with the team. Stop to sign the book in the heavy box at its base. This is also a good place to look right across Craiglyn Dyfi, the lake which is the source of the Afon Dyfi, and to photograph the Aran range.

On your left as you climb up to Aran Fawddwy's ridge is the site of a war-time aircrash. A photo-reconaissance Mosquito crashed here whilst on a cross-country exercise on 9th February, 1944. The plane was based at RAF Benson (Oxon) with 540 squadron and had survived 16 sorties over Europe. The wreckage was finally found on 14th February, 1944, with the dead bodies of both the Polish pilot and the British navigator. A year and a day after this crash, a Bristol Beaufighter crashed below Aran Fawddwy's summit on 10th February, 1945. It was based at Pershore with No 1, Ferry Unit. In snow and ice, both the Australian pilot and the British navigator were killed instantly. In between these crashes, on 16th September, 1944, a Republic P-47 Thunderbolt dived into Aran Fawddwy near its summit, killing the pilot.

There is a huge cairn on Aran Fawddwy's summit, reputedly built by the men of Mawddwy when they heard that Cadair Idris was just a few feet higher than their mountain. They could have saved their energy as Aran Fawddwy is a good 43 ft higher than its more famous rival — it is also the highest mountain in Britain south of the Snowdon ridge. Its summit affords some excellent views, with Llyn Tegid (Bala Lake), the largest natural lake in Wales, to the north (just to your left as you look along the ridge from Aran Fawddwy to Aran Benllyn, with Arenig Fawr (2800 ft) to its left. Sweeping left (westwards) you may just see the 3560 ft summit of Snowdon on the horizon, while the bumps of the Rhinogs (highest point Y Llethr, 2475 ft) run like a reptile's spine down to the Mawddach estuary, giving you a glimpse of sand on a clear day if the tide is out. Even further round to the left are Cadair Idris (2928 ft) and Pumlumon (2468 ft), in the south. On your right are the Berwyns and Offa's Dyke. A splendid place on a fine day!

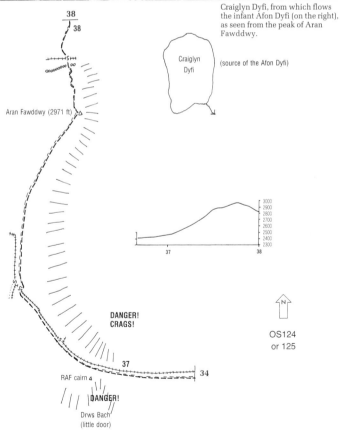

Craiglyn Dyfi, from which flows
the infant Afon Dyfi (on the right),
as seen from the peak of Aran
Fawddwy.

Craiglyn
Dyfi

(source of the Afon Dyfi)

Aran Fawddwy (2971 ft)

DANGER!
CRAGS!

OS124
or 125

N

37

34

RAF cairn

DANGER!

Drws Bach
(little door)

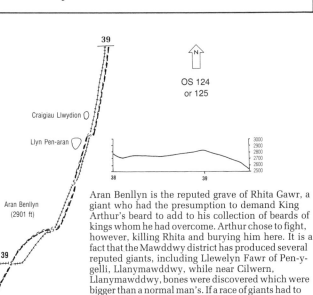

Aran Benllyn is the reputed grave of Rhita Gawr, a giant who had the presumption to demand King Arthur's beard to add to his collection of beards of kings whom he had overcome. Arthur chose to fight, however, killing Rhita and burying him here. It is a fact that the Mawddwy district has produced several reputed giants, including Llewelyn Fawr of Pen-y-gelli, Llanymawddwy, while near Cilwern, Llanymawddwy, bones were discovered which were bigger than a normal man's. If a race of giants had to seek a remote sanctuary, why not this area? There *were* giants on the earth in those days ...

Looking along the ridge from Aran Fawddwy to Aran Benllyn, with Bala Lake in the background.

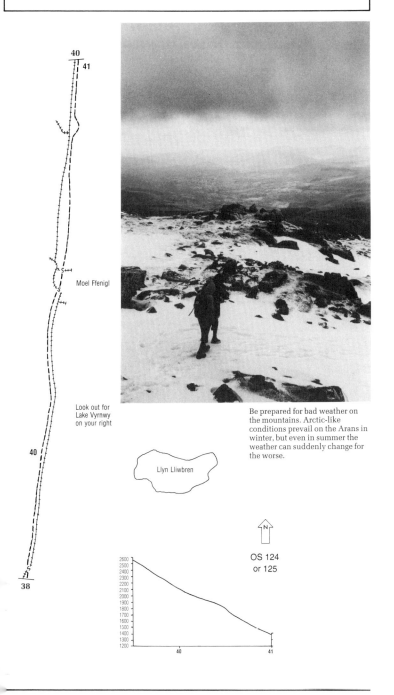

40
41

Moel Ffenigl

Look out for
Lake Vyrnwy
on your right

40

38

Be prepared for bad weather on
the mountains. Arctic-like
conditions prevail on the Arans in
winter, but even in summer the
weather can suddenly change for
the worse.

Llyn Lliwbren

N

OS 124
or 125

2600
2500
2400
2300
2200
2100
2000
1900
1800
1700
1600
1500
1400
1300
1200

40   41

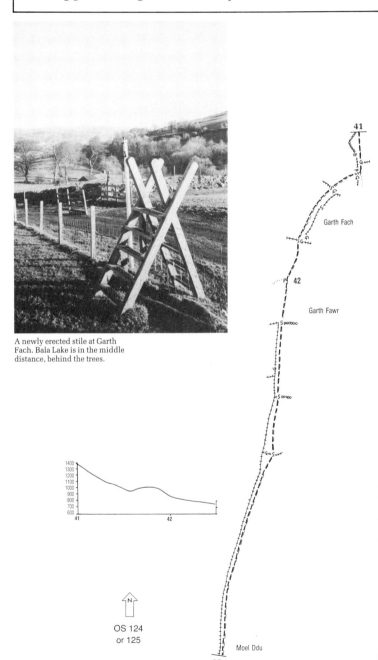

A newly erected stile at Garth Fach. Bala Lake is in the middle distance, behind the trees.

41

Garth Fach

42

Garth Fawr

OS 124
or 125

Moel Ddu

39

The Bala Lake Railway at
Llanuwchllyn, complete with the
canopy from Aberdyfi station.

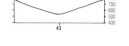

Take a break from the walk at Llanuwchllyn to ride
the Rheilffordd Llyn Tegid (Bala Lake Railway) along
the lake side to Bala, where there is a campsite near
the station, a youth hostel and bed and breakfast
accommodation, plus all the facilities of a small town,
including a Snowdonia National Park Visitor Centre
in the High Street. If you miss the train, there is also
a bus service, while Llanuwchllyn has its own shops
and a nearby campsite. The present 1ft 11½ ins
narrow gauge line which covers the 4½ miles to Bala
is laid on the bed of the old standard 4ft 8½ ins gauge
track, which carried trains from the old Barmouth
Junction (now Morfa Mawddach) to Ruabon from
1868 until flooding near Penmaenpool heralded its
closure in 1965. The Bala Lake Railway reopened this
most scenic section in stages from 1972 to 1976.
Llanuwchllyn station canopy was actually brought
here from Aberdyfi when that station was
downgraded to a halt, so if you came to Wales by
train, now you know here it went! Just over a mile
to the north of Llanuwchllyn is Caer Gai, the Roman
fort which is where King Arthur spent his youth with
his foster-brother, Sir Cai. A nearby farm is
intriguingly named Llys Arthur (Arthur's Palace —
map reference SH861286). Spencer referred to
Arthur's upbringing here in his *'Faery Queen'*:

> 'His dwelling is, low in a valley green,
> Under the foot of Rauran mossy hole'
> (Rauran is Aran).

The Llanuwchllyn area has been the home of some
great Welsh patriots and advocates of the Welsh
language, including Sir Owen Morgan Edwards. His
son, Sir Ifan ab Owen Edwards, founded the first all
Welsh school in 1939 and the Urdd Gobaith Cymru
(Welsh League of Youth) in 1922.

Campsites at Bryn Gwyn Farm
Llanuwchllyn, *T* 06784 272 &
Penybont Touring Park, Bala,
T 0678 520549.
Bala youth hostel, *T* 0678 520215.
Plenty of B&B, inc. Plas Teg Guest House,
Bala, *T* 0678 520268

OS124 or 125

LLANUWCHLLYN
(Bus, train, shops, B&B)

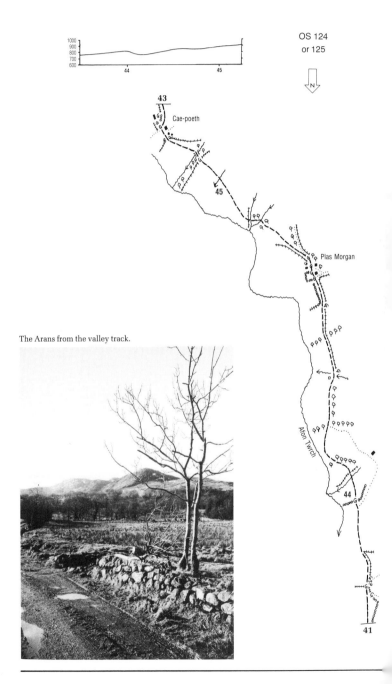

OS 124
or 125

The Arans from the valley track.

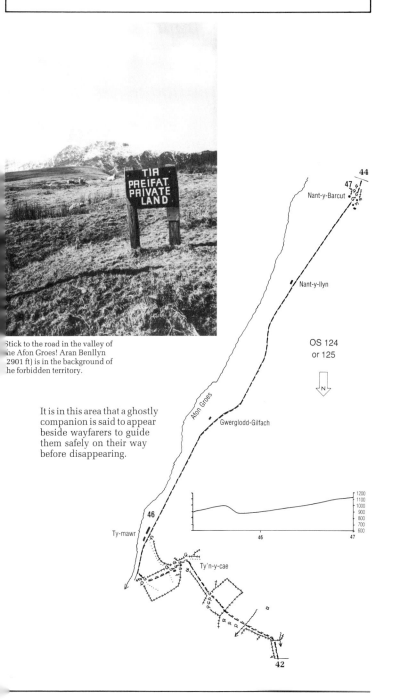

Stick to the road in the valley of the Afon Groes! Aran Benllyn (2901 ft) is in the background of the forbidden territory.

It is in this area that a ghostly companion is said to appear beside wayfarers to guide them safely on their way before disappearing.

Nant-y-Barcut

Nant-y-llyn

OS 124
or 125

N

Afon Groes

Gwerglodd-Gilfach

Ty-mawr

Ty'n-y-cae

Aran Benllyn (2901 ft), seen from
Cwm-ffynnon.

Cwm-Ffynnon

Afon Groes

OS 124
or 125

Aran Fawddwy and the valley of
the infant Afon Dyfi, where it is
known as the Llaethnant or 'milk
stream'.

The Dyfi is here called the Llaethnant
(llaeth: milk) because of its milky white
foam in this rocky, upper stretch from
Craiglyn Dyfi. A maid of St Tydecho is said
to have dropped some milk whilst crossing
here. Instead of scolding her, Tydecho
converted the whole river into milk at this
point for the benefit of the poor at a time of
great scarcity. A depression overlooking the
Llaethnant is Ffynnon Dydecho (Tydecho's
Well), while his bed, Gwely Tydecho, is a
shelf in a nearby rock.

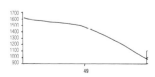

46 Bryn Hall

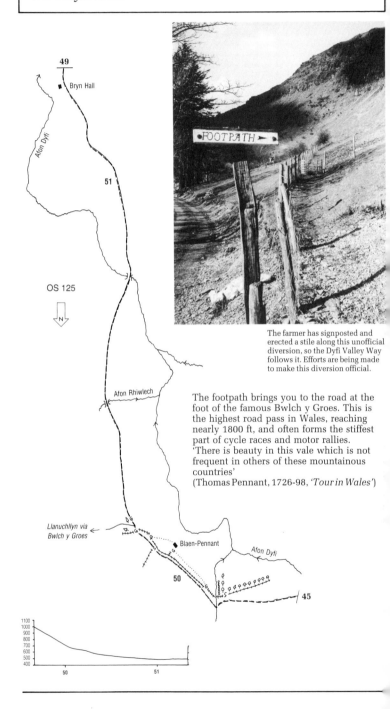

The farmer has signposted and erected a stile along this unofficial diversion, so the Dyfi Valley Way follows it. Efforts are being made to make this diversion official.

The footpath brings you to the road at the foot of the famous Bwlch y Groes. This is the highest road pass in Wales, reaching nearly 1800 ft, and often forms the stiffest part of cycle races and motor rallies. 'There is beauty in this vale which is not frequent in others of these mountainous countries' (Thomas Pennant, 1726-98, *'Tour in Wales'*)

OS 125

49
Bryn Hall

Afon Dyfi

51

Afon Rhiwlech

Llanuchllyn via ← Bwlch y Groes

Blaen-Pennant

Afon Dyfi

50

45

St Tydecho's church,
Llanymawddwy.

Watch out for a white horse as you approach Bryn Hall. A local lad was once shown a mystery by a ghostly rider here, while visiting motorists have stopped for his white horse, only for it to vanish before their eyes The ghost seems to be connected with a foul deed at Bryn Hall, where there is a bloodstain on the stairs which defies all attempts to remove it, including changing the wooden boards. It is believed to be the blood of a murdered baby whose mother was a chambermaid but whose father was the estate owner. The ghostly rider is probably the wicked father riding to hide the murdered baby's body in the woods. It is also said that the house can shake violently.

Llanymawddwy is the spiritual centre of Mawddwy and you should make a point of visiting St Tydecho's church. This has long been a holy spot and its Christian nature probably predates St Tydecho, since a tombstone c 500 AD was found here. Its Latin inscription translates as '(the stone) of the daughter of Salvianus. Here (she) lies, Ve ....maie, wife of Tigirnicus, and of his daughter Rigohene. She lies (here), wife of Oneratus...'

The burial of Salvianus himself is recorded at Caer Gai, near Llanuwchllyn, where a stone c 500 AD was dug up with this inscription (in Latin): 'Here lies Salvianus Bursocavi(s), sone of Cupetianus'. Could he be related to Sir Cai, Arthur's foster-brother?

Arthur's nephew, Tydecho, is the saint whose church stands at Llanymawddwy today. Tydecho was the brother of St Samson and a first cousin to St Cadfan. One of three leaders of saints from Brittany to Wales, Tydecho was renowned for his austerity, wearing a hair coat and sleeping on rock.

That great tormentor of saints, Maelgwn Gwynedd (Arthur's Sir Lancelot), thought one day he would annoy the saint by sending a stud of white horses to be pastured by his prayers. Tydecho turned them loose on the mountainside and they were found to be fat, despite the conditions. Maelgwn, provoked by this, seized the saint's oxen while at team. The next day, however, wild deer, in place of the oxen, were seen ploughing the land (Dol y Ceirw, near the Dyfi) with a grey wolf harrowing after them, so Maelgwn sent a pack of hounds to chase them away and sat down on the blue stone of Tydecho to watch the sport. When he attempted to rise, he found himself stuck to the rock and had to humbly beg the saint's pardon to be freed. On being released, he returned Tydecho's oxen and atoned by giving him the privilege of sanctuary for 'a hundred ages' — asylum for man and beast and exemption from all fighting, burning and killing.

Pistyll Gwyn, the aptly named 'white spout' waterfall, is the reason for this route's diversion up and down Cwm Dyniewyd. The water drops at least 100 feet down the bare rock face and an interesting side view is possible. Near the base of the waterfall are the remains of an old lime kiln and settling beds, while further down the valley is evidence of mid 19thC mining and more recent early 20thC use of water-power.

The high ground above the sheer dead-end of Cwm Dyniewyd was the scene of a fatal aircrash. At 1.12 pm on April 6th, 1942 a Mark 1C Vickers Wellington bomber (serial number P9299) belonging to 1429 Flight, took off from its base at East Wretham on a cross-country training flight. The all Czech pupil crew flew into low cloud, causing them to fly up this valley to their tragic end. All six crew members were killed in the crash.

Photo: Overlooking the Dyfi Valley at Dinas Mawddwy from Cefn-Coch.

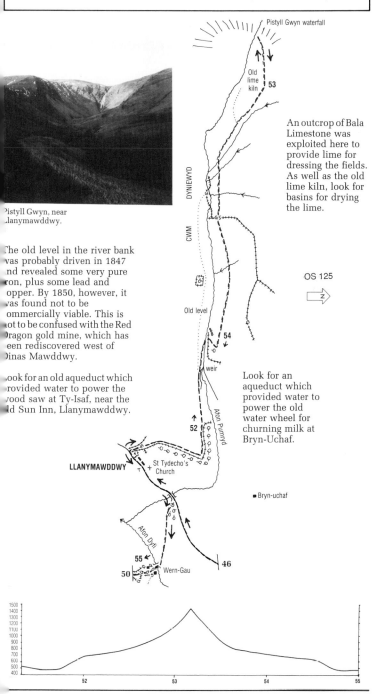

Pistyll Gwyn waterfall

Old lime kiln **53**

DYNIEWYD

CWM

An outcrop of Bala Limestone was exploited here to provide lime for dressing the fields. As well as the old lime kiln, look for basins for drying the lime.

OS 125

Old level

54

weir

Afon Pumryd

52

LLANYMAWDDWY

St Tydecho's Church

Bryn-uchaf

55

50

Wern-Gau

46

Look for an aqueduct which provided water to power the old water wheel for churning milk at Bryn-Uchaf.

Pistyll Gwyn, near Llanymawddwy.

The old level in the river bank was probably driven in 1847 and revealed some very pure iron, plus some lead and copper. By 1850, however, it was found not to be commercially viable. This is not to be confused with the Red Dragon gold mine, which has been rediscovered west of Dinas Mawddwy.

Look for an old aqueduct which provided water to power the wood saw at Ty-Isaf, near the Old Sun Inn, Llanymawddwy.

Afon Dyfi

1500 1400 1300 1200 1100 1000 900 800 700 600 500 400

52   53   54   55

50 Coed-Cae

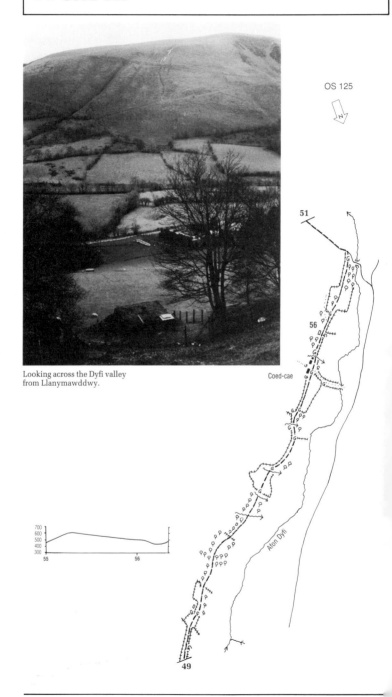

N

51

56

Coed-cae

Afon Dyfi

Looking across the Dyfi valley
from Llanymawddwy.

49

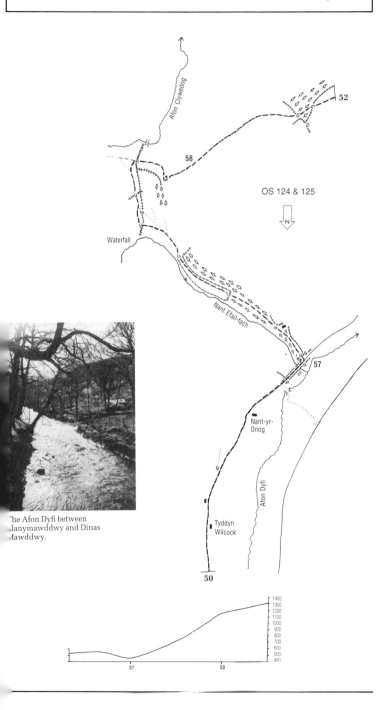

Afon Clywedog

52

58

OS 124 & 125

N

Waterfall

Nant Efail-fach

57

Nant-yr-Onog

Afon Dyfi

Tyddyn Wilcock

50

The Afon Dyfi between Llanymawddwy and Dinas Mawddwy.

1400
1300
1200
1100
1000
900
800
700
600
500
400

57

58

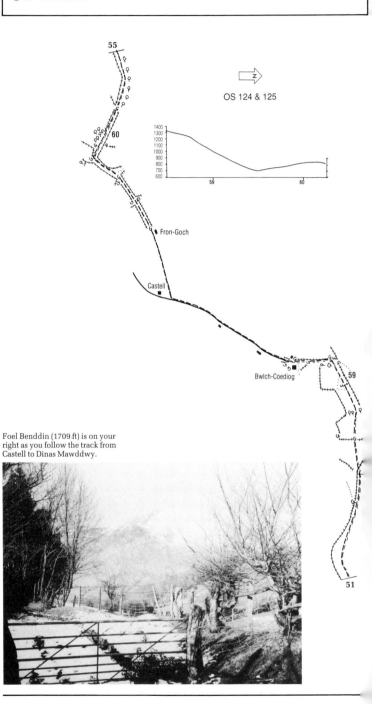

52 Castell

OS 124 & 125

55

60

Fron-Goch

Castell

Bwlch-Coediog

59

51

Foel Benddin (1709 ft) is on your right as you follow the track from Castell to Dinas Mawddwy.

Castell.

Castell is an interesting name for a farmhouse. The place is famous for its ghost rather than for a castle, however. It is said that a woman owned this property whose husband visited a mistress elsewhere. When the wife died the husband used the dead woman's hand to forge her will. Later, when her husband was entertaining in the house, a maid went to a locked cabinet to take out her former mistress' favourite crockery. She recoiled in horror when a ghostly hand appeared to stop her unlocking the cabinet door. Other evidence of ghostly activity were cows refusing to enter a cowshed, an apparition of a white cat, furniture shaking and strange sounds in a particular bedroom. Eventually the family decided to leave for another farmhouse. They had loaded the wagon with furniture but the horses wouldn't pull it. It wasn't until their dead mistress' favourite teapot was taken from the load that the wagon moved. For a long time it was considered necessary to take back anything that was borrowed from the house on the same day that it was borrowed.

Pont Minllyn, the 17thC Packhorse bridge over the Afon Dyfi.

Back in Dinas Mawddwy, our route this time gives a close-up view of the 17thC packhorse bridge Pont Minllyn. It stands between the old railway station, now a wholefood café, and Celyn-Brithion campsite. The Mawddwy railway had a troubled history from 1867, when a Government Inspector refused it a certificate. Passenger services were temporarily closed in 1901 because of lack of repair of equipment, followed by complete closure in 1908. Absorption into the Cambrian Railway brought a grand re-opening in 1911, however, soon to be justified by the war traffic to the ammunition which was then stored in Minllyn slate quarry. The end of hostilities did not bring a resumption in the slate industry, however, while buses were to provide competition for the passenger traffic from 1924. As a result, passenger services finished in 1930, although the combined Dovey Valley Sunday Schools' excursion to Aberystwyth ran annually in June until 1939. The second world war kept the line open for goods, with the quarry warehouse used to store machinery for the Rover Car Company. As with the Corris Railway, however, damage to a bridge over the Dyfi led to the line's closure in 1951. The line never paid a single dividend to its shareholders in the 83 years of its existence (the last freight train actually ran on 5th September, 1950) and the track had been lifted by a contractor from Sheffield by May 1952. The station trackbed can be seen near Pont Mallwyd. It is unfortunate that the Mawddwy Railway disappeared just a few years before the era of the 'Great Little Trains' for tourists to Wales.

Meirion Mill, Dinas Mawddwy.

The café in the old railway station
at Dinas Mawddwy.

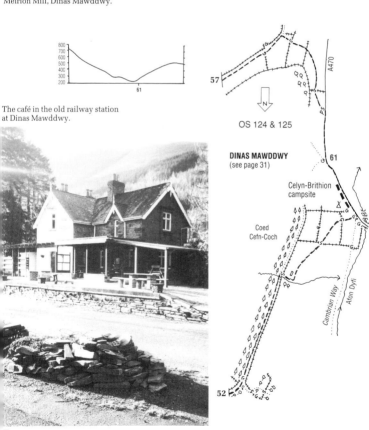

OS 124 & 125

DINAS MAWDDWY
(see page 31)

Celyn-Brithion
campsite

Coed
Cefn-Coch

Cambrian Way

Afon Dyfi

A470

Old mammoth bones adorn the porch of St Tydecho's church, Mallwyd.

George Borrow found Mallwyd a small but pretty village, noting that Dr John Davies was a former rector of its ancient church. One of the greatest of Welsh scholars, he published a Welsh Grammar in 1621 and a Welsh-Latin Dictionary in 1632, while reputedly checking Bishop Parry's translation of the Bible into Welsh. Dr Davies' wife was a granddaughter (on her mother's side) of Baron Lewis Owen, who was murdered by the Red Bandits of Mawddwy, from whom Mallwyd's Brigands Inn is named (see page 58). Mallwyd is probably derived from Maen Llwyd, or standing stone, presumably where the church now stands. The church was sited here, and not on higher ground, through supernatural intervention. Its porch, dated 1641, is adorned with old bones, probably of a prehistoric mammoth, dug up here.

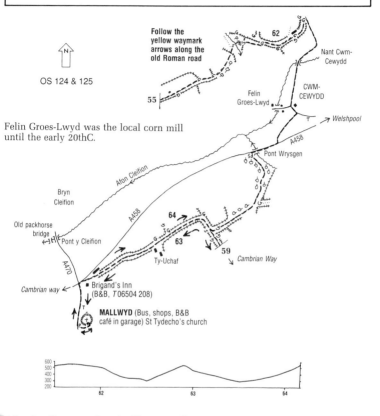

OS 124 & 125

Follow the
yellow waymark
arrows along the
old Roman road

Felin Groes-Lwyd was the local corn mill
until the early 20thC.

Follow the yellow arrows along the old Roman road between Cae'r Gof and Cwm-Cewydd.

58 Collfryn

It is worthwhile making the short detour from this route to the burial mound, obscured by trees, near Collfryn. This is where the Red Bandits of Mawddwy (Gwylliaid Cochion Mawddwy) were buried in 1555, some 441 years after their formation in 1114. Their first leader was Owain, son of Cadwgan, son of Bleddyn, who incurred the wrath of Henry I of England in 1107 when he kidnapped Nest, the beautiful daughter of Rhys ap Tewdwr and wife of Gerald of Windsor, custodian of Pembroke Castle. Owain was a prince of Powys and Nest was King Henry's former concubine and the mother of his illegitimate son, the Duke of Gloucester, whose legitimacy would have avoided the war of succession between Stephen and Matilda. Nest was famed for her beauty and her easily transferable affections. Her abduction by Owain was intolerable to the English, however, who used the excuse to threaten war, and to the Welsh, who saw the affair endangering their fragile independence. Owain took Nest to Plas Eglwyseg, near Llangollen, but it appears that Nest spent some time in Dinas Mawddwy, which was then in Powys. A shop in the village is still called Nant Nest Stores, as it is sited where Nest's house stood — the view from its garden can explain why Nest is said to have loved this spot best of all. Owain was forced to flee to Ireland, however, leaving Nest to make her way back to Pembroke. He returned in 1114 with a band of outlaws from Ireland. Owain died in the fight that ensued their landing in Pembrokeshire but his outlaws ended up here. 'Gwylliaid' is derived from 'gwyll' (dusk), when they started on their thefts. They were given the epithet 'cochion' either because they had ruddy skin or red hair (or both) or because their hands were red with blood. Mawddwy was virtually an independent outlaw state for over 400 years. They were experts with bows and arrows and were famed for travelling for great distances along the branches of trees without touching the ground. They were finally dealt with by the strong new authority of the Tudors. Baron Lewis Owen, of Plas Court, Dolgellau, and John Wynn, son of Meredydd of Gwydir, were authorised to punish the clan for their crimes. They came to the bandits' stronghold at Dugoed on Christmas Eve 1554, and captured over 80 of them. Among them was Jac Goch, whose mother pleaded that he be pardoned. When Baron Lewis Owen refused, she bared her breasts and said 'these yellow breasts have given suck to those who shall wash their hands in your blood'. Enough bandits remained to carry out this vow of revenge. When the baron next passed this way he was ambushed at a place called Llidiart y Barwn.

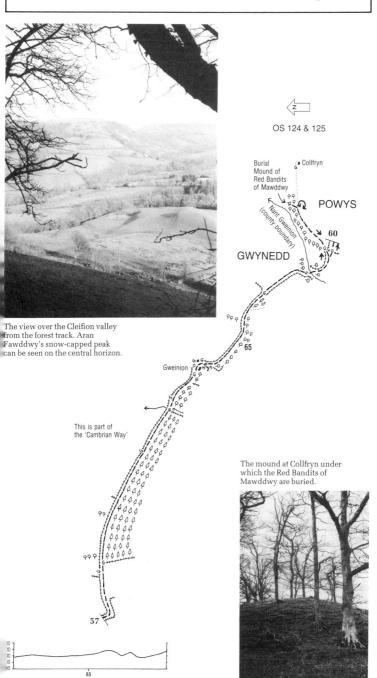

OS 124 & 125

Burial
Mound of
Red Bandits
of Mawddwy

Collfryn

POWYS

Nant Gweinion
(county boundary)

GWYNEDD

60

65

Gweinion

This is part of
the 'Cambrian Way'

The view over the Cleifion valley
from the forest track. Aran
Fawddwy's snow-capped peak
can be seen on the central horizon.

57

The mound at Collfryn under
which the Red Bandits of
Mawddwy are buried.

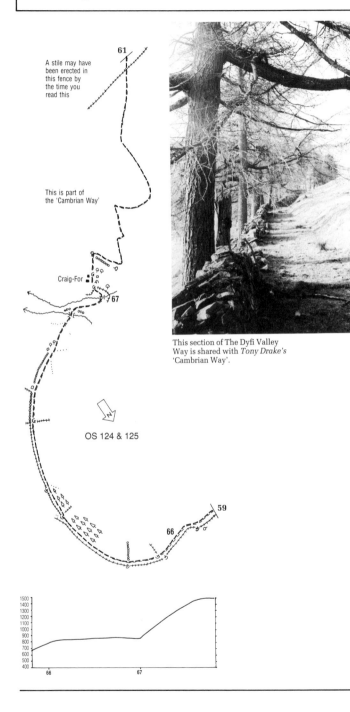

61

A stile may have been erected in this fence by the time you read this

This is part of the 'Cambrian Way'

Craig-For

67

59

66

OS 124 & 125

N

This section of The Dyfi Valley Way is shared with *Tony Drake's* 'Cambrian Way'.

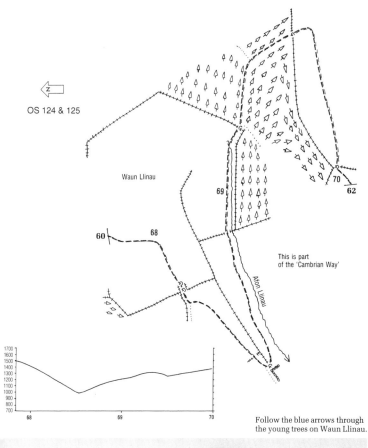

OS 124 & 125

Waun Llinau

69

60 | **68**

70

62

This is part
of the 'Cambrian Way'

Afon Llinau

Follow the blue arrows through
the young trees on Waun Llinau.

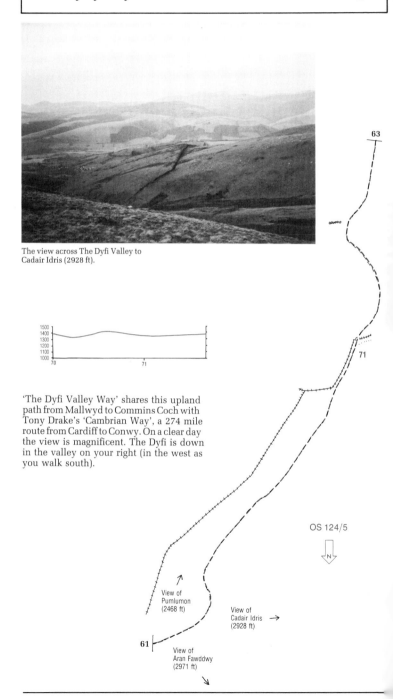

The view across The Dyfi Valley to
Cadair Idris (2928 ft).

'The Dyfi Valley Way' shares this upland
path from Mallwyd to Commins Coch with
Tony Drake's 'Cambrian Way', a 274 mile
route from Cardiff to Conwy. On a clear day
the view is magnificent. The Dyfi is down
in the valley on your right (in the west as
you walk south).

63

71

OS 124/5

N

View of
Pumlumon
(2468 ft)

View of
Cadair Idris →
(2928 ft)

61

View of
Aran Fawddwy
(2971 ft)

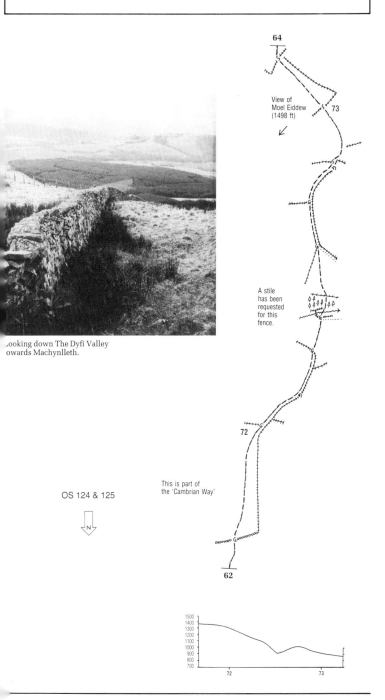

64

View of
Moel Eiddew
(1498 ft)
↙

73

A stile
has been
requested
for this
fence.

72

This is part of
the 'Cambrian Way'

OS 124 & 125

↓N

62

Looking down The Dyfi Valley
towards Machynlleth.

1500
1400
1300
1200
1100
1000
900
800
700

72   73

This simple signpost does little to suggest that this well trodden path is shared by The Dyfi Valley Way, the Cambrian Way, and Glyndŵr's Way.

65

Cambrian Way

74

'Glyndŵr's Way'
to Machynlleth

Cemmaes

P

Gwalia
(B&B *T* 06502 377
Vegans and vegetarians
catered for)

This waymarked path is
used by three long-distance
paths: 'The Dyfi Valley Way',
the 'Cambrian Way' and
'Glyndŵr's Way', a 120 mile
route from Knighton to
Welshpool via Machynlleth
and named after the great
Welsh patriot, Owain
Glyndŵr.

1000
900
800
700
600
500
400
300

74

'Glyndŵr's Way'
to Welshpool

63

OS 135
or 136

The Way has been waymarked with yellow arrows from Commins Coch to Cefncoch-Uchaf. The yellow arrows continue to waymark a short circular walk down the hill to Glantwymyn (Cemmaes Road), however.

'Glyndŵr's Way' is also, confusingly, waymarked with yellow arrows. In time, it is hoped to waymark 'The Dyfi Valley Way' with a distinctive dove emblem.

The access path to the standing stone at Cefncoch-Uchaf is not a right of way. The farmer has kindly given permission for the waymarked stile and courtesy path, where you walk at your own risk.

'The Dyfi Valley Way' says farewell to the 'Cambrian Way' at Commins Coch, only to resume its brief contact with 'Glyndŵr's Way'.

The 'Cambrian Way' will hopefully soon be waymarked with a distinctive Welsh top hat emblem.

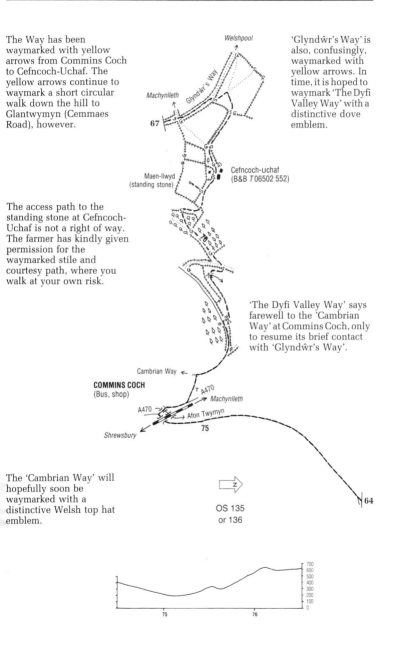

Welshpool

Glyndŵr's Way

Machynlleth

67

Maen-llwyd
(standing stone)

Cefncoch-Uchaf
(B&B *T* 06502 552)

Cambrian Way ←

COMMINS COCH
(Bus, shop)

A470
Machynlleth

A470
Afon Twymyn

75

Shrewsbury

OS 135
or 136

64

700
600
500
400
300
200
100
0

75   76

The standing stone at Cefncoch uchaf. Notice how its tip is shaped like the distant silhouette of Fron Goch the holy hill towards which it points.

The standing stone that you pass at Cefncoch Uchaf is about 3 ft 9 ins high and 7 ft 6 ins in circumference. It is one of three stones that used to mark a sanctuary or 'Noddfa'. A second, larger, stone stands at Tal-y-wern (see page 68)

OS 135 or 136

69

The track from Cefncoch uchaf to
Darowen, with Fron Goch (945 ft)
in full view.

Cefn (B&B
T 06502 336)

+ **DAROWEN**
(Postbus)

77

65

The name Darowen is
assumed to mean
Owen's Oak. The
circular graveyard
around St Tudyr's
church suggests an
ancient site, although
the present building
was completed in 1864.
St Tudyr is buried here
and on his festival,
October 15th, a young
man used to be carried
around the parish on
his companions'
shoulders while others
beat him with sticks,
perhaps in memory of
some persecution
endured by the saint.

800
700
600
500
400
300
200
100
0

77

The standing stone at Tal-y-wern.

The standing stone near Tal-y-wern is over 6 ft high and 12 ft 6 ins in circumference, and stands in the centre of 'cae yr hen eglwys' (old church field). The remains of an old church were found in this field near the stone, thus reinforcing the view that it was an ancient holy site taken over by the early Christians. This appears to be the 'male' stone to the smaller 'female' stone at Cefncoch-Uchaf (page 66). A third stone once stood to the east of Darowen and was called Carreg y Noddfa. The 'Archaeologica Cambrensis' of 1856 refers to 'the township of Noddfa, the name of which implies a place of refuge, or a sanctuary, its limits being properly described by three stones'. There is a local tradition of the stones giving sanctuary. Suspected wrongdoers would be given a head start in a race to the stone and would go free if they won. The easy transition to a Christian site may indicate how the druids embraced the new religion early in the Christian era (cf *'Celt, Druid and Culdee'* by Elder and *'The Drama of the Lost Disciples'* by Jowett). It is possible, too, that these stones mark leys or earth energy lines. The road going east from Tal-y-wern is an old drove road, reminding us of the days when the Welsh economy depended on droving herds of cattle to market in England.

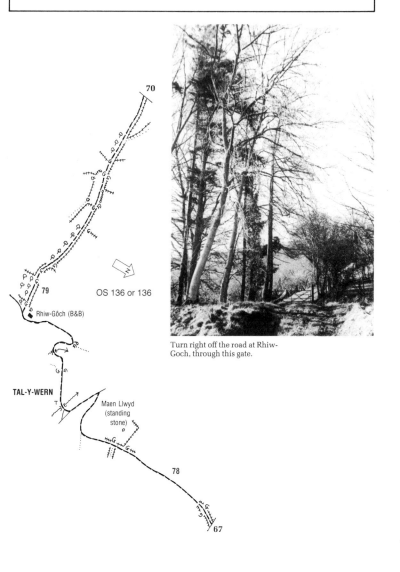

OS 136 or 136

79

◆ Rhiw-Gôch (B&B)

TAL-Y-WERN

Maen Llwyd
(standing
stone)

78

70

67

Turn right off the road at Rhiw-
Goch, through this gate.

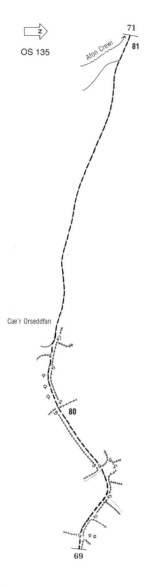

OS 135

71
81

Afon Crewi

Cae'r Orseddfan

80

69

The new footbridge over the river
Crewi at Rhiwfelen.

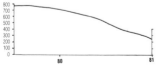

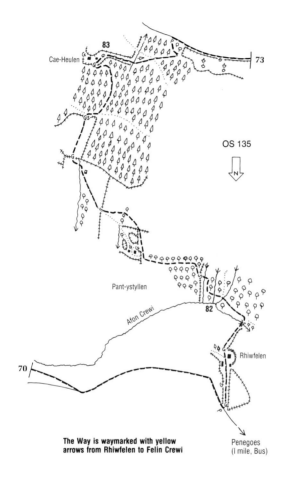

Cae-Heulen

83

73

OS 135

N

Pant-ystyllen

Afon Crewi

82

Rhiwfelen

70

**The Way is waymarked with yellow
arrows from Rhiwfelen to Felin Crewi**

Penegoes
(I mile, Bus)

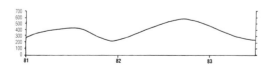

The award winning restored working water mill of Felin Crewi is another of the highlights of this walk. Plan to reach here at a mealtime so that you can enjoy food, made with Felin Crewi's own stoneground flour, in the adjoining café. The old mill was lovingly restored by Mr & Mrs Partridge in the mid 1980s after being disused since the 1940s, when cheaper flour from centralised and faster roller mills made water milling uneconomical. With the demand for more flavoursome and nutritious wholemeal flour increasing, however, a few such mills have made successful comebacks. Oats and wheat are ground, while barley would have been popular when the local farmers depended on this mill for their animal feed. The corn mill has been sited on the banks of the river Crewi since the 18thC, although the original water-wheel would have been smaller than its replacement. A wooden mill race fed the mill pond with water from the weir. A fulling mill or pandy was situated here before the corn mill, as indicated by the name of the cottage on the corner of the approach road. Fulling meant thickening the woollen cloth to make it weatherproof. Until the 1300s this was achieved by treading on it in urine to shrink it. Later this work was done with wooden mallets driven by a water-wheel. Visitors are welcome to inspect the restoration, while a bird hide is just one outside attraction. Felin Crewi is open every day from Easter to the end of September from 10.30 am to 6.00 pm, while you can see just the mill working from Mondays to Fridays during the winter. The licensed evening restaurant is open on Fridays and Saturdays from July to September, and Sunday lunches are available between mid-day and 2.00 pm. Telephone 0654-3113.

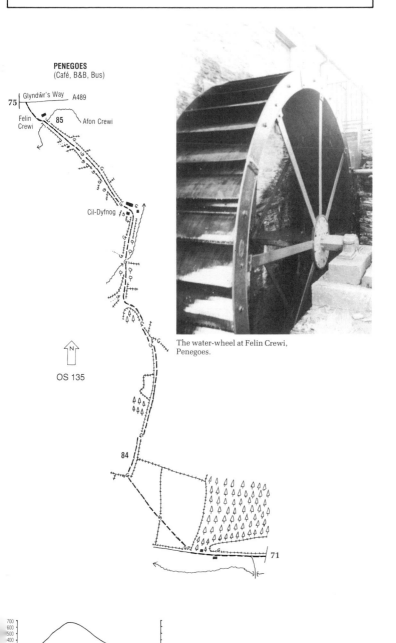

PENEGOES
(Café, B&B, Bus)

Glyndŵr's Way   A489
75
Felin
Crewi   85   Afon Crewi

Cil-Dyfnog

N

OS 135

The water-wheel at Felin Crewi,
Penegoes.

84

71

700
600
500
400
300
200
100
0
        84   85

The holy wells, or St Cadfarch's springs, at Penegoes.

Penegoes is said to mean 'Head of Egoes', after the legendary Celtic chieftain whose head is reputedly buried beneath a grove of oak trees beyond the church. Was this, like the burial of bran's head under the Tower of London, geomantic protection or rule after death? The head cult was deeply rooted in pagan Celtic practices (although Bran, whose story features in *'The Mabinogion'*, is credited with introducing Christianity to Britain). Detached heads were valued and venerated, evidently as links with the spirit world, and it can be reasonably assumed that in each case the spirit directly concerned was the former owner of the head. The church was founded by St Cadfarch, a descendant of Old King Cole, or Coel, in the mid 6thC, although the present building was erected in 1863. Across the old Roman road from the church are the holy wells or springs which are named after St Cadfarch, and which were lovingly restored by the Machynlleth & District Civic Society in 1984. Look for a slate step up from the road, near a tree which has a plaque fixed to it. If you suffer from rheumatism the water is reputed to bring relief! Penegoes is also the birthplace of the artist Richard Wilson, born in the Rectory in 1713. Wilson became an early and brilliant landscape painter whose paintings now hang in the National Gallery. He died at Mold (Clwyd) in 1782.

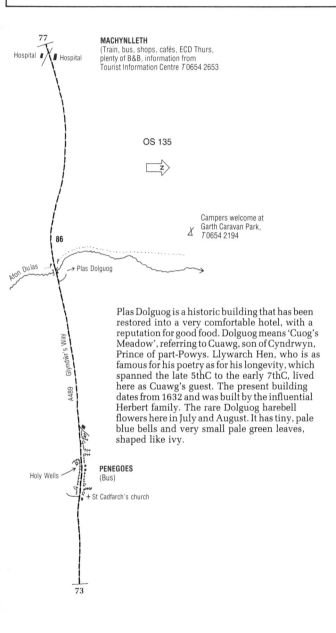

MACHYNLLETH
(Train, bus, shops, cafés, ECD Thurs,
plenty of B&B, information from
Tourist Information Centre *T* 0654 2653

77

Hospital ▮ ▮ Hospital

OS 135

Campers welcome at
Garth Caravan Park,
T 0654 2194

86

Afon Dulas ... → Plas Dolguog

Glyndŵr's Way

A489

Plas Dolguog is a historic building that has been
restored into a very comfortable hotel, with a
reputation for good food. Dolguog means 'Cuog's
Meadow', referring to Cuawg, son of Cyndrwyn,
Prince of part-Powys. Llywarch Hen, who is as
famous for his poetry as for his longevity, which
spanned the late 5thC to the early 7thC, lived
here as Cuawg's guest. The present building
dates from 1632 and was built by the influential
Herbert family. The rare Dolguog harebell
flowers here in July and August. It has tiny, pale
blue bells and very small pale green leaves,
shaped like ivy.

Holy Wells → **PENEGOES**
(Bus)

+ St Cadfarch's church

73

200
100
0

86

The best way to appreciate Machynlleth's role as the market town of the Dyfi Valley is to come here on a Wednesday. To walk down Maengwyn Street is to enter a colourful, bustling street market which has endured since King Edward I granted the Lord of Powys a charter in 1291 to hold a market at Machynlleth for ever (plus two fairs a year). This charter was issued less than ten years after Edward's conquest of Wales. Machynlleth can lay claim to much more, however, for it was here that the great patriot Owain Glyndŵr was crowned before representatives from France, Scotland and Castile as the last native independent Prince of Wales. He held his first parliament in 1404 at a spot near the modern Mid Wales Tourist Information Centre. This excellent source of tourist information, which houses a display on the Dyfi Valley, is part of the Owain Glyndŵr Institute. The building on its left is the Parliament House. While the Tourist Information Centre is a mock late medieval Welsh town house, the Parliament House, which houses an exhibition on Owain Glyndŵr, is genuinely old and may be the building that Glyndŵr used. It is at least in the right place. No wonder that when Jan Morris had a vision of a modern independent Wales in the Interlude of her book *'The Matter of Wales'*, she made Machynlleth its capital. Her President of the Republic lived in the mansion Plas Machynlleth, once the home of the Marquess of Londonderry. Lord Randolph Churchill (father of Sir Winston Churchill) was the nephew of the Fifth Marquess, Henry Vane-Tempest, and he visited frequently. Royalty also came here before the Plas and its grounds were presented to the town of Machynlleth after World War II. Your route passes the Londonderry family portrait gallery on the ground floor, before continuing past the children's playground.

Photo: The Plas, Machynlleth.

Owain Glyndŵr's Parliament
House, Machynlleth.

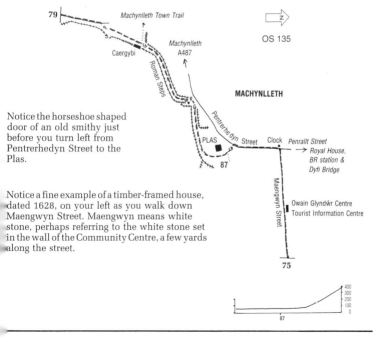

Notice the horseshoe shaped
door of an old smithy just
before you turn left from
Pentrerhedyn Street to the
Plas.

Notice a fine example of a timber-framed house,
dated 1628, on your left as you walk down
Maengwyn Street. Maengwyn means white
stone, perhaps referring to the white stone set
in the wall of the Community Centre, a few yards
along the street.

The Roman Steps may indeed have been cut by the Romans. Machynlleth's own claim to fame as being the Roman Maglona has been disputed through lack of archaeological evidence, but the Roman fort at Pennal (Cefn Caer) probably did have a look-out post on this hill, Wylfa. The local mineral wealth was being exploited in Roman times and there may have been a track to the lead mines of Dylife

The railway has been important to Machynlleth ever since its enthusiastic opening in January 1863, when 1500 passengers marched in procession to Machynlleth station for a special train, hauled by two locomotives, to Newtown and back. The right turn to the station at Machynlleth's Clock Tower makes a worthwhile diversion, taking you past the Royal House on your left and on to the Dyfi Bridge, uniting Powys and Gwynedd. Dafydd Gam, who owed great personal loyalty to King Henry IV, attempted to assassinate Owain Glyndŵr in Machynlleth and was reputedly imprisoned in Royal House. Charles I is also connected with this very old building, although he probably failed to keep an appointment to sleep there in 1644. The distinctive Clock Tower was erected to mark the coming of age of Charles Stewart Vane-Tempest, Viscount Castlereagh, in 1873. Tourism is now one of the mainstays of the local economy, and will be given a further boost when the new sport and leisure centre, to be built by the Plas, is completed.

Photo: The Roman Steps, Machynlleth.

The view over Machynlleth.

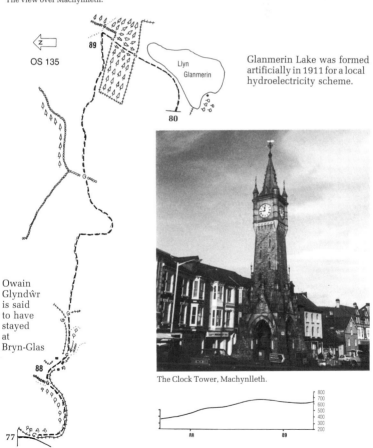

OS 135

Llyn Glanmerin

Glanmerin Lake was formed artificially in 1911 for a local hydroelectricity scheme.

Owain Glyndŵr is said to have stayed at Bryn-Glas

The Clock Tower, Machynlleth.

80 Glanmerin

Glanmerin.

81

91

Nant Rhisglog

Glanmerin

90

Don't go through this gate after
Glanmerin! Follow the yellow
arrow.

OS 135

N

79

The Llyfnant valley marks the boundary between Powys and Dyfed. It was once an important highway, with timber, bark, hides and wool brought down it to the old port of Derwenlas.

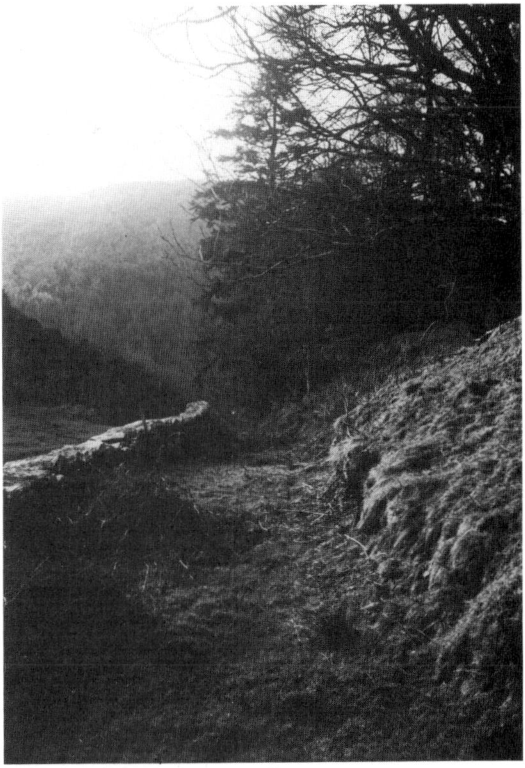

The track approaching the Llyfnant valley.

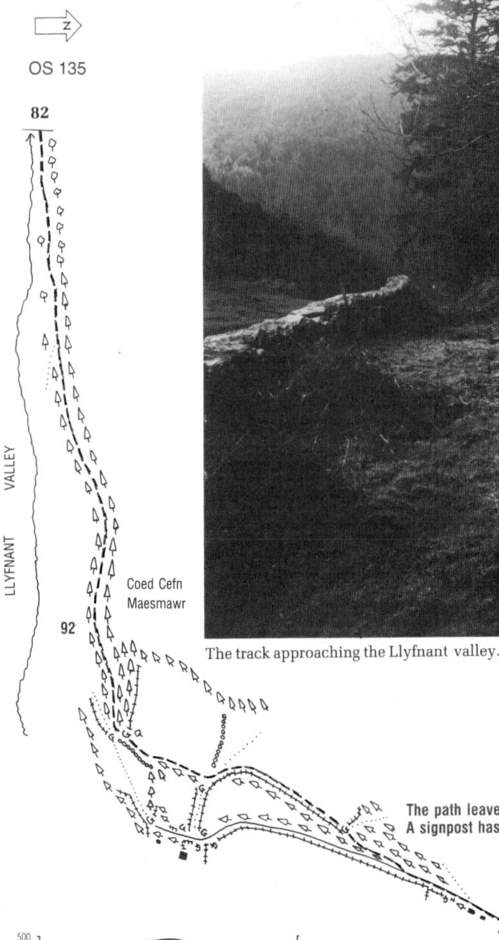
N
OS 135
82
LLYFNANT VALLEY
Coed Cefn Maesmawr
92
The path leaves the road at the quartz boulder. A signpost has been requested for here
80

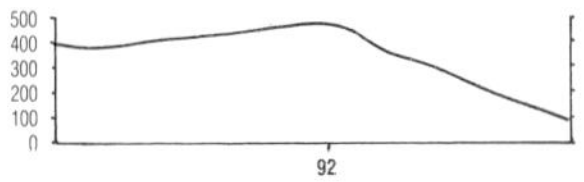
500
400
300
200
100
0
92

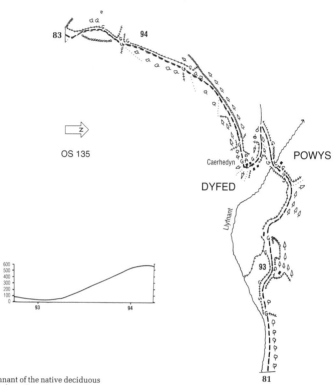

OS 135

POWYS

Caerhedyn

DYFED

Llyfnant

A remnant of the native deciduous
forest above Cymerau.

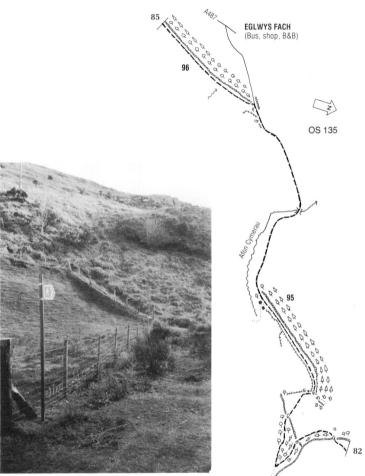

85

A487

EGLWYS FACH
(Bus, shop, B&B)

96

OS 135

Afon Cymerau

95

82

Turn left off the road at this public
footpath signpost just before
Eglwys Fach.

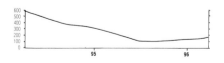

Furnace derives its name from the disused water powered furnace which used to be part of an important iron works. This has been restored and is now open to the public. The charcoal-burning blast furnace was built circa 1755, taking advantage of the charcoal provided by the local woodland. Its proximity to the coast allowed the easy use of imported iron ore from Cumbria. The water-wheel was used to power bellows which created the necessary draught for the very high temperatures needed to smelt iron. The furnace was abandoned in 1810 and was later converted into a sawmill. The nearby waterfall is in Cwm Einion, or Artists' Valley. It has attracted painters for over a century.

The waterfall at Furnace.

Sarn Helen, the old Roman road,
makes a fine track between
Furnace and Beth Taliesin.

OS 135

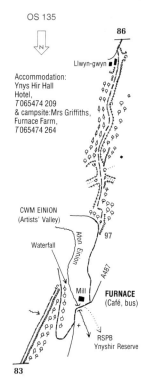

86

Llwyn-gwyn

Accommodation:
Ynys Hir Hall
Hotel,
T 065474 209
& campsite:Mrs Griffiths,
Furnace Farm,
T 065474 264

CWM EINION
(Artists' Valley)

Afon Einion

97

Waterfall

A487

Mill

FURNACE
(Café, bus)

RSPB
Ynyshir Reserve

83

The view over the Dyfi estuary
from Sarn Helen, near Bedd
Taliesin.

Sarn Helen is an ancient causeway which
runs from Carmarthen in south Wales to
Caerhun (near Conwy) in north Wales.
Although such raised roads were known in
Ancient Britain and ascribed to Molmutius
and his son Belinus (c. 400 BC), this one is
usually dated to the Romans. Helen has
been identified as the British wife of
Magnus Maximus, the Macsen Wledig of
the '*Mabinogion*' who made a bid for the
purple (reserved for the emperor of Rome)
in 383 AD. Another Helen is the British
mother of Constantine the Great. Both of
these Helens lived long after the Roman
forts that are strung along this route were
constructed, however, so the Helen (Elen)
may be a corruption of Lleng, meaning
legion. It could even be a corruption of
halen (sea salt). Our route from Furnace to
Bedd Taliesin is probably part of Sarn
Helen, with this section affording a fine
view over the Dyfi estuary on your right,
while the Victorian ruins of the Bryndyfi
lead mine lie across the fields on your left.

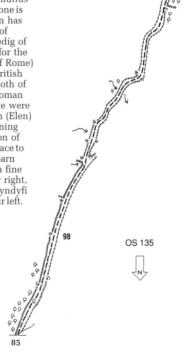

87

99

Lletyr Ffron

98

OS 135

N

85

Bedd Taliesin.

Bedd Taliesin is reputedly the grave of the 6thC bard Taliesin, a contemporary of Arthur and Merlin and ranking with them in greatness. It is said that it is unlucky to disturb these ancient barrows and when some people dug here in the 19thC they provoked thunder and lightning, causing them to flee. Taliesin was found as a baby in a coracle caught in a fish weir at nearby Borth by Elphin, a local prince. When he grew up he was to return the favour by rescuing Elphin from Deganwy Castle. Taliesin features in the '*Mabinogion*', the great Welsh contribution to medieval European literature, as the 'Chief of Bards'.

'Their Lord they shall praise,
Their language they shall keep,
Their land they shall lose
Except Wild Wales.'

Taliesin: *Destiny of the Britons.*

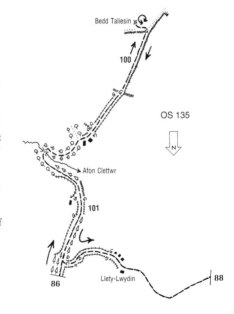

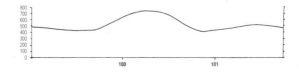

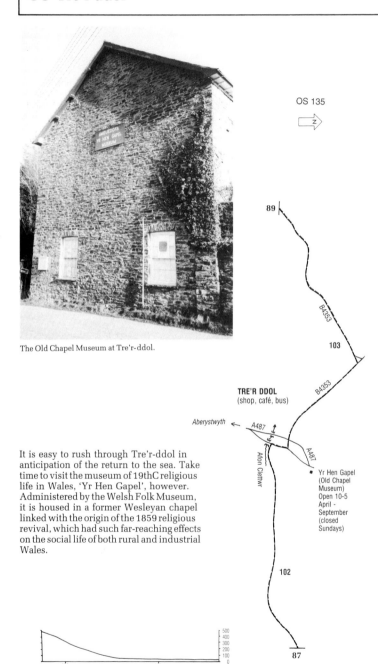

The Old Chapel Museum at Tre'r-ddol.

OS 135

It is easy to rush through Tre'r-ddol in anticipation of the return to the sea. Take time to visit the museum of 19thC religious life in Wales, 'Yr Hen Gapel', however. Administered by the Welsh Folk Museum, it is housed in a former Wesleyan chapel linked with the origin of the 1859 religious revival, which had such far-reaching effects on the social life of both rural and industrial Wales.

89

B4353

103

B4353

TRE'R DDOL
(shop, café, bus)

Aberystwyth ←   A487

A487

Afon Clettwr

Yr Hen Gapel
(Old Chapel
Museum)
Open 10-5
April -
September
(closed
Sundays)

102

87

OS 135

Ty-Mawr campsite
T 097081 327 △

90

△ Penpontbren campsite
T 097081 392

105

B4353

Cynfelyn was the son of Bleiddud, the son of Meiriawn, the son of Tybiawn, the son of Cunedda Wledig, who came down from north of Hadrian's Wall to drive out the Irish invaders and reassert British rule in north Wales in the early 5thC. He lived here as a hermit. Sarn Cynfelyn, the 7 mile causeway running out to sea from between Borth and Aberystwyth, is also named after the saint.

The road at Llancynfelyn church.

Ty-Craig
campsite
T 097086 339 △

104

+ Llancynfelyn

88

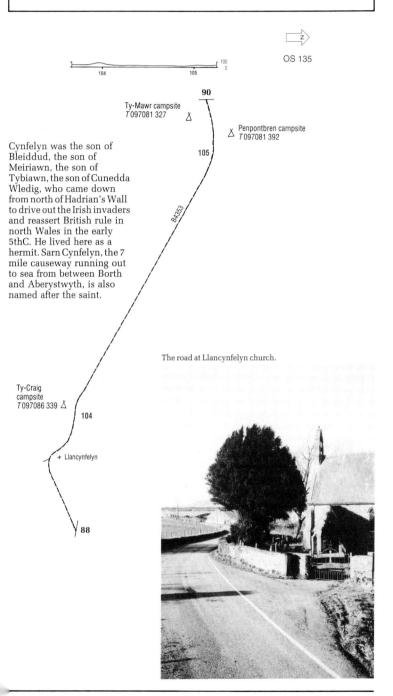

The great tradition of boat building is maintained at Ynyslas. The river Leri was even diverted away from the sea and into the Dyfi estuary in 1842 so that a wharf could be built to take advantage of sheltered moorings.

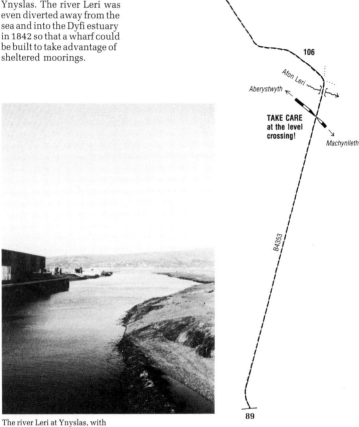

OS 135

91

YNYSLAS

106

Afon Leri

Aberystwyth ←

TAKE CARE at the level crossing!

Machynlleth ↘

B4353

89

100
0

106

The river Leri at Ynyslas, with Aberdyfi across the estuary.

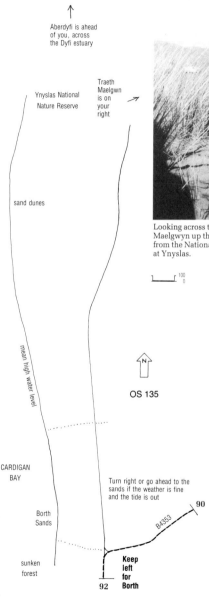

↑

Aberdyfi is ahead
of you, across
the Dyfi estuary

Ynyslas National
Nature Reserve

Traeth
Maelgwn
is on
your
right ↗

sand dunes

mean high water level

CARDIGAN
BAY

Borth
Sands

sunken
forest

Turn right or go ahead to the
sands if the weather is fine
and the tide is out

**Keep
left
for
Borth**

92

90

B4353

Looking across the sands of Traeth
Maelgwyn up the Dyfi estuary
from the National Nature Reserve
at Ynyslas.

⊢————⌐ 100
⌐ 0

↑N

OS 135

A visit to the Ynyslas National
Nature Reserve is an optional (but
highly recommended) extra.
From it, during the summer, you
could complete this route by ferry
back to the start at Aberdyfi.
Alternatively, walk into Borth
along the sands. Ynyslas National
Nature Reserve freely admits the
public. It has an Information
Centre, a nature trail and rare
flora and fauna. Traeth Maelgwn
is the beach where Maelgwn
Gwynedd (King Arthur's Sir
Lancelot) had himself elected
Pendragon, or head war-lord,
after Arthur's death. As ruler of
Gwynedd, he met here with the
rulers of Deheubarth (Dyfed) and
Powys (the three modern counties
of Gwynedd, Dyfed and Powys
still meet near here) for a test. The
winner would be the one who
could sit longest in his chair as
the tide rose. Maelgwn had his
chair prepared with wax wings so
that it floated. The event is re-
enacted as part of the annual
Borth Carnival at the end of
September, with the winner
crowned king by an attendant
druid.

**FINISH AT BORTH
RAILWAY STATION,**
map reference,
SN 609901

108

↓
Machynlleth

▲
Youth
Hostel
T 0970
81498

Don't forget to finish with a paddle
in the sea at Borth!

107   108

CARDIGAN
  BAY

BORTH (Train, bus, shops, Café,
ECD Wed, plenty of B&B,
youth hostel *T* 0970 81498 & camp sites

OS 135

N

107

B4353

mean high water level

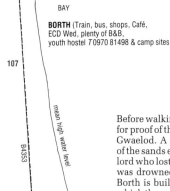

Borth
Sands

sunken
forest

91

Before walking towards Borth, inspect the seashore
for proof of the legend of the drowning of Cantre'r
Gwaelod. A sunken forest can be seen rising out
of the sands exposed at spring tides. Gwyddno, the
lord who lost his rich land when Cantre'r Gwaelod
was drowned, ended up as a fisherman at Borth.
Borth is built on a long, narrow, shingle bank
which the sea flows under to the bogland behind.
Easy access to a fine four mile long beach has made
Borth an interesting resort, served by British Rail.
It was the railway's arrival in 1863 that caused
Borth to develop from a tiny fishing hamlet. Now
it provides the comfort of the 'Cambrian Coast
Express' straight through to London Euston in 5
hours (with stops, including Shrewsbury and
Birmingham).

Walking the Way — transport and accommodation

If you are a diehard backpacker and long-distance walker you can skip these pages. All you need to know is that you can take a train to the start at Aberdyfi and from the finish at Borth, and that there are campsites or other means of accommodation at reasonable intervals for a day's walk, as indicated on page 5 and detailed at the appropriate places on the strip map. This little extra is for ordinary mortals who fear for their comfort. The motorist has a great advantage when it comes to walking in rural Wales. The use of a car allows the flexibility usually denied by the sparse nature of public transport. The Dyfi Valley Way crosses roads regularly enough to enable motorists to divide it into convenient sections. It's even better if you can play the 'two car trick' with a friend, to avoid walking back to where you parked. Instead, leave car A at your destination and drive together in car B from it to your start, returning together in car A to car B. You can cut out short lengths of road walking and divide the Way into the following sections:

Aberdyfi — Pennal (8 miles); Pennal — Pantperthog (8 miles); Corris — Aberangell (8 miles); Aberangell — Cwm Cywarch (7 miles); Cwm Cywarch — Llanuwchllyn (9 miles); Llanuwchllyn — Blaen Pennant (7 miles); Llanymawddwy — Pistyll Gwyn & back (3 miles); Llanymawddwy — Mallwyd (8 miles); Mallwyd — Gwalia (11 miles); Commins Coch — Caer Orseddfan (5 miles); circular south of Penegoes via Rhiwfelen (4 miles); Machynlleth — Furnace (10 miles); Furnace — Tre'r-ddol (5 miles).

Motorists are allowed to cheat by driving the final 6 miles to Borth, but they *must* paddle in the sea on arrival.

Public transport is not what you may be used to in other parts of Britain, but it *does* exist. Gwynedd County Council in particular are to be congratulated on their promotion of the Bws Gwynedd network. Send a large sae for a timetable, leaflets and map to: The County Planning Department, County Council Offices, Caernarfon, Gwynedd, LL55 1SH. Most buses are operated by Crosville, who will send you their map and timetable leaflets (covering Powys and Dyfed as well as Gwynedd). Send a large sae to: Crosville Wales Ltd, Imperial Buildings, Glan-y-mor Road, Llandudno Junction, Gwynedd, LL31 9RH.

There is a full range of accommodation along this route. In addition to those places listed, addresses are available from the Mid Wales Tourist Information Centre, Canolfan Owain Glyndŵr, Machynlleth, Powys, SY20 8EE. They can provide other tourist information as well. Machynlleth is a good base from which to walk The Way, using public transport. This is fairly easy between Aberdyfi and Aberllefenni, but take care to reach Dinas Mawddwy when a bus runs (currently Wednesdays and Saturdays to Machynlleth and all Fridays, school days and Thursdays in the summer holidays to Dolgellau — for connections to Machynlleth or Llanuwchllyn). Commins Coch has a regular weekday bus service to Machynlleth, while Darowen has a weekday afternoon post bus. Regular buses link Tre'r-ddol and Furnace with Machynlleth, while The Way finishes at Borth railway station for the train back to Machynlleth.

If you aren't a member of the Youth Hostels Association but would like to use their hostels at Corris, Bala or Borth, you can obtain membership details from the YHA, Trevelyan House, 8 St Stephen's Hill, St Alban's, Herts, Al1 2DY.

Suggested one week trip

Avoid carrying heavy pack over Aran Fawddwy (2971 ft) By leaving tent at Dinas Mawddwy campsite (stay overnight at Bala Youth Hostel before returning to Dinas Mawddwy).

Fri   Arrive Aberdyfi by train. B&B.
Sat   Walk to Pantperthog campsite.
Sun   Walk to Dinas Mawddwy campsite.
Mon   Walk to Llanuwchllyn for train or bus to Bala.
Tue   Early bus from Bala to Llanuwchllyn for walk back to Dinas Mawddwy base camp.
Wed   Walk to B&B near Commins Coch or Darowen.
Thur   Walk to Machynlleth campsite.
Fri   Walk to Llancynfelyn campsite.
Sat   Walk to Borth for train home.

Index

96 Key to strip maps

——15—	The footpath route, with distance walked from the start in miles
··········	Other paths
———	Motor roads
▬▭▬	British Rail line
┼┼┼	Hedge or fence
∞∞∞	Wall
▯	Standing stone
∘°∘	Stone circle
G	Gate
S	Stile
P	Metal signpost
w	Wooden waymark post
⌇⟶	Stream or river, with direction of flow
⊣E⟶	Bridge
⋰⋰	Earthwork
△	Peak
\\\\///	Steep, dangerous, crags
♤♤♧♧	Trees
▪◾▰	Buildings
㕉	Ruin
+	Church or chapel
T	Telephone box
▲	Youth hostel
⇌	British Rail station
OS 135	Relevant Ordnance Survey Landranger sheet number
⬃	Direction of north

Each map has a profile of the walk showing the height in feet above sea level and the distance in miles from the start.

Afon is Welsh for river, nant means stream.

0 Scale in miles	

Laurence Main is the Ramblers' Association's voluntary footpaths secretary for the districts of Meirionnydd and Montgomery. If you are interested in joining the Ramblers Association, please write for full details to:
The Ramblers' Association, 1/5 Wandsworth Road, London, SW8 2XX
(large sae. please).